THE WETHERILLS

FRIENDS OF MESA VERDE

By
Fred M. Blackburn

ISBN 1-887805-21-4

Author
Fred M. Blackburn

Mesa Verde Centennial Series Editor
Andrew Gulliford

Content and Copy Editor
Elizabeth A. Green

Design and Layout
Lisa Snider Atchison

Mesa Verde Centennial Series Editorial Committee
Lisa Snider Atchison, Tracey L. Chavis,
Elizabeth A. Green, Andrew Gulliford, Tessy Shirakawa,
Duane A. Smith and Robert Whitson

Printed in Korea

To Mom and Dad, Keith and Sylvia

who taught me the value of culture and to observe

in the world of natural and cultural history.

*We knew that if we did not break into that charmed world
someone else would, sometime – someone who might not love and respect
those emblems of antiquity as we did. It was a strange feeling:
perhaps all this had been given into our keeping
until someone else might do it
more capably than we.*

– Al Wetherill (circa 1950)

A message from the Superintendent of Mesa Verde National Park

Our centennial celebrates an important moment in Mesa Verde National Park's history. It is an opportunity to share stories of what led to establishment of the park on June 29, 1906, and its designation as a World Heritage Cultural Site in 1978. This is a time to reflect upon its past and share hopes and visions for the next 100 years.

As Mesa Verde National Park nears its 100th birthday, it is important to remember that the archaeological sites it protects have been here far longer. Their survival is a credit to the skilled Ancestral Puebloan masons who created them 700 to 1600 years ago.

Following the Puebloan people's migration south to the Rio Grande area around 1300, the Utes continued to occupy the Mesa Verde area. They remain today and were responsible for the protection and preservation of Mesa Verde prior to its establishment as a national park. The park and the American public owe much to all these surviving indigenous people.

More than 100 years before its establishment as a national park, non-native people began exploring and documenting the archaeological sites at Mesa Verde, including Spanish explorers, geologists, ranchers, miners, photographers, naturalists, and archaeologists. They shared the story of fantastic stone cities in the cliffs, attracting more and more visitors to the area.

Prior to 1914, the 25-mile trek from Mancos Canyon to Spruce Tree House took an entire day, traveling the first 15 miles by wagon and the next 10 miles on foot or by horseback. This included a nearly vertical climb to the top of Chapin Mesa. Today more than one-half million people visit Mesa Verde National Park each year – a considerable increase over the 100 visitors documented in 1906.

"Leaving the past in place" is just one of the unique ideas pioneered at Mesa Verde. In 1908, when archaeology mainly consisted of collecting artifacts for distant museums, Jesse Walter Fewkes repaired, but did not rebuild, Spruce Tree House for visitation. He documented the excavation and created a small museum to house its artifacts. That tradition is continued today and Mesa Verde is recognized worldwide as a leader in non-invasive archaeology – studying and documenting sites without shovels to disturb the past. With the involvement of the 24 tribes affiliated with Mesa Verde and ongoing research, we continue to learn more about the stories that Mesa Verde National Park preserves.

Our centennial will celebrate 100 years of preservation and honor all who have gone before us. This centennial book series was created to tell some of their stories, of discovery, travel, transportation, archaeology, fire and tourism. These stories have contributed to our national heritage and reinforce why we must continue to preserve and protect this national treasure for future generations.

Enjoy the celebration. Enjoy the book series. Enjoy your national park.

– Larry T. Wiese

About the Mesa Verde Museum Association

Mesa Verde Museum Association (MVMA) is a nonprofit, 501 (c) 3 organization, authorized by Congress, established in 1930, and incorporated in 1960. MVMA was the second "cooperating association" formed in the United States after the Yosemite Association. Since its inception, the museum association has provided information that enables visitors to more fully appreciate the cultural and natural resources in Mesa Verde National Park and the southwestern United States. Working under a memorandum of agreement with the National Park Service, the association assists and supports various research activities, interpretive and education programs, and visitor services at Mesa Verde National Park.

A Board of Directors sets policy and provides guidance for the association. An Executive Director assures mission goals are met, strengthens partnerships, and manages publishing, education, and membership program development. A small year-round staff of five, along with more than 15 seasonal employees, operates four sales outlets in Mesa Verde National Park and a bookstore in Cortez, Colorado. The association carries nearly 600 items, the majority of which are produced by outside vendors. MVMA currently publishes approximately 40 books, videos, and theme-related items, and more than 15 trail guides.

Since 1996 MVMA has been a charter partner in the Plateau Journal, a semi-annual interpretive journal covering the people and places of the Colorado Plateau. In addition, the association has been a driving force in the Peaks, Plateaus & Canyons Association (PPCA), a region-wide conference of nonprofit interpretive associations. PPCA promotes understanding and protection of the Colorado Plateau through the publication of joint projects that are not feasible for smaller associations.

Mesa Verde Museum Association is also a longtime member of the Association of Partners for Public Lands (APPL). This national organization of nonprofit interpretive associations provides national representation with our land management partners and highly specialized training opportunities for board and staff.

Since 1930 the association has donated more than $2 million in cash contributions, interpretive services, and educational material to Mesa Verde National Park. MVMA's goal is to continue enhancing visitor experience through its products and services, supporting vital park programs in interpretation, research and education.

Visit the online bookstore at mesaverde.org and learn more about Mesa Verde National Park's centennial celebration at mesaverde2006.org. Contact MVMA offices for additional information at: telephone 970-529-4445; write P.O. Box 38, Mesa Verde National Park, CO 81330; or email info@mesaverde.org.

The Center of Southwest Studies

The Center of Southwest Studies on the campus of Fort Lewis College in Durango, Colorado, serves as a museum and a research facility, hosts public programs, and strengthens an interdisciplinary Southwest college curriculum. Fort Lewis College offers a four-year degree in Southwest Studies with minors in Native American Studies and Heritage Preservation. The Center includes a 4,400-square-foot gallery, the Robert Delaney Research Library, a 100-seat lyceum, and more than 10,000 square feet of collections storage. The new $8 million Center of Southwest Studies building is unique among four-year public colleges in the West, because the facility houses the departments of Southwest Studies and Anthropology, and the Office of Community Services, which helps Four Corners communities with historic preservation and cultural resource planning.

The Colorado Commission on Higher Education has recognized the Center of Southwest Studies as a "program of excellence" in state-funded higher education. Recent gifts to the Center include the $2.5 million Durango Collection ®, which features more than eight hundred years of southwestern weavings from Pueblo, Navajo and Hispanic cultures.

The goal of the Center is to become the intellectual heart of Durango and the Southwest and to provide a variety of educational and research opportunities for students, residents, scholars and visitors. Strengths in the Center's collections of artifacts include Ancestral Puebloan ceramic vessels, more than 500 textiles and dozens of southwestern baskets. The Center's holdings, which focus on the Four Corners region, include more than 8,000 artifacts, 20,000 volumes, numerous periodicals, and 500 special collections dating from prehistory to the present and with an emphasis on southwestern archaeology, maps, and original documents. These collections include more than two linear miles of manuscripts, unbound printed materials, more than 7,000 rolls of microfilm (including about 3,000 rolls of historic Southwest region newspapers), 600 oral histories, and 200,000 photographs. Contact the Center at 970-247-7456 or visit the Center's website at swcenter.fortlewis.edu. The Center hosts tours, educational programs, a speakers' series, and changing exhibits throughout the year.

Center of Southwest Studies website: http://swcenter.fortlewis.edu

About the publisher

The publisher for the Mesa Verde Centennial Series is the Ballantine family of Durango and the Durango Herald Small Press. The Ballantine family moved to the Four Corners region in 1952 when they purchased the *Durango Herald* newspaper.

Durango has a magnificent setting, close to the Continental Divide, the 13,000-foot San Juan Mountains, and the 500,000-acre Weminuche Wilderness. The Four Corners region encompasses the juncture of Colorado, Utah, Arizona, and New Mexico, the only place in the nation where four state borders meet. Residents can choose to ski one day in the San Juans and hike the next day in the wilderness canyons of southeast Utah. This land of mountains and canyons, deserts and rivers is home to diverse Native American tribes including the Southern Utes, Ute Mountain Utes, Jicarilla Apache, Hopi, Zuni, and the Navajo, whose 17-million-acre nation sprawls across all four states. The Four Corners is situated on the edge of the Colorado Plateau, which has more national forests, national parks, national monuments, and wilderness areas than anywhere else on earth.

Writing and editing the newspaper launched countless family expeditions to Ancestral Puebloan sites in the area, including spectacular Mesa Verde National Park, the world's first park set aside for the preservation of cultural resources in 1906 to honor America's indigenous peoples. The Ballantine family, through the *Durango Herald* and the *Cortez Journal,* have been strong supporters of Mesa Verde National Park and Fort Lewis College.

Arthur and Morley Ballantine started the planning for the Center of Southwest Studies at Fort Lewis College in 1964 with a $10,000 gift. In 1994 Morley began the Durango Herald Small Press, which publishes books of local and regional interest. The Press is proud to be a part of the 100th birthday celebration for Mesa Verde National Park.

Durango Herald Small Press website: www.durangoheraldsmallpress.com

From left: Joel Brisbin, Bruce Bradley, Larry Nordby, Fred Blackburn and Frank Shields documenting inscriptions in Spruce Tree House.

ACKNOWLEDGMENTS

Without the foresight and continued review for accuracy provided by members of the Wetherill and Mason families, this publication would not be possible. The Wetherill Family Archives, entrusted to the Bureau of Land Management's Anasazi Heritage Center in Dolores, Colorado, provided a foundation for research. I wish to thank the Jane Marcher Foundation, Bob and Beverly Bartner and Sherman Loy for helping fund this endeavor. Additional documents and oral histories were obtained from the Wetherill family, my archives and research, numerous institutions, oral histories, and more than 2,000 published citations related to this branch of the Wetherill family. All resources were used to clarify the Wetherill family's unique story. Every care was made to accurately reflect source material. Any errors or oversights are the responsibility of the author.

Wetherill and Mason family acknowledgments: Pat Chounard, Johni Lou Duncan, Chris Dunkleberger and family, Isabel Eaton, Marietta Eaton, Dorothy Leake, Harvey Leake, Delbert and Richard Lilly, Frances

(Fanny) Mahan, Jimmy and Marie Schaffner, Sue Swinehart, Carol Ann Getz, Bob Getz, Lynn Getz, William John Wetherill, Samantha Wetherill, Tom Wetherill, Wren Wetherill Scarberry, and Tom and Jan Wade Vaughan. All of them maintain the pioneering spirit of their ancestors.

Primary documents, whenever possible, were the basis for fact checking, thanks to the talents of many editors, scholars, and those who undertake the drudgery of database and fieldwork. Among those in the background are Kay Barnett, Joel Brisbin, Linda Martin, Larry Nordby, Paul Rogers, and Cynthia Williams Loebig of the Mesa Verde site assessment team, as well as research archivist Carolyn Landes. Larry Nordby deserves special thanks for giving me the opportunity of a lifetime, placing his trust in me and allowing me access within Mesa Verde National Park archaeological sites to record historic inscriptions. Kay Barnett was my recording partner over a period of three years, cross-checking interpretation and catching my mistakes. Paul Rogers, a phenomenal archivist, teamed with me in the search of southwestern archives. Robert Jensen and Bob Fitzgerald aided with digital and film reproduction of photographs for this text. Volunteer assistance by Jefferson County Open School students and staff of Lakewood, Colorado, especially lead teacher Jeff Bogard, is very much appreciated. Winston Hurst, Harvey Leake, James Knipmeyer, and John Richardson have all been stalwart reviewers and critics of the work. Without the efforts of John Richardon, many historic photographs would have been missed. Andrew Gulliford, Morley Ballantine, and Duane Smith provided encouragement, mentorship and advice to pursue this publication. Julia Johnson inspired and directed the Wetherill/Grand Gulch Project, providing the opportunity for inscription documentation. Lynn Robertson spent countless thoughtful hours compiling from the Wetherill Family Archives a collection genealogy. Charlie and Ivy Gaines shared the journal of Richard Gaines. Allan Nossaman's most detailed historical treatise of the history of Silverton, Colorado, was of great help.

Marty Costos and Carol Dunsworth helped with photocopying and data entry work in the collection. Russell Heaton and Ray Williamson helped with understanding the Society of Friends.

I wish to thank J. Marilyn Dobson and Shirley Kennedy for providing permission to excerpt from the journal of Leander F. Hayes. Judith Reynolds provided me with valuable information and insights into Gustaf Nordenskiöld's explorations and excavations with the Wetherills.

Special appreciation is due Patricia Flint Lacey, and Beth Green whose quiet and firm support combined with exacting editorial skills to help compile my research into a readable document.

Special thanks to all of those who have played large and small parts in support of the Wetherill Family Archives; you know who you are.

Last, but not least, special thanks to my wife Victoria Atkins, who ably assisted with editing, and children Lucas and Julianna, who face the brunt of grumpiness when I'm writing.

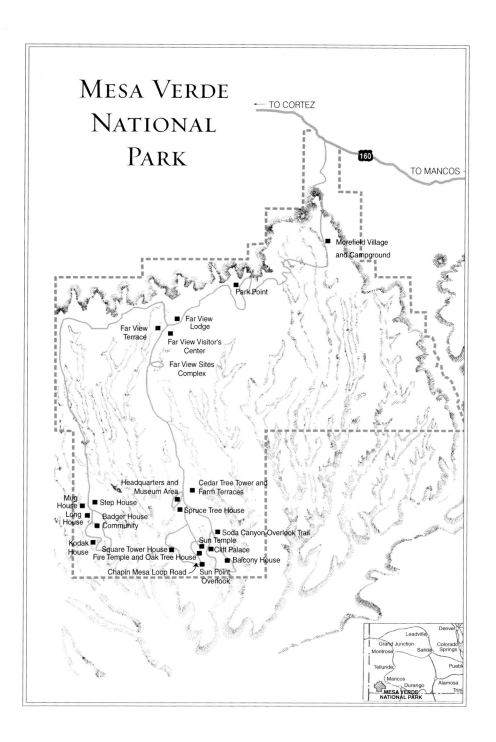

MESA VERDE
NATIONAL
PARK

← TO CORTEZ

160

TO MANCOS

Morefield Village
and Campground

Park Point

Far View
Lodge

Far View
Terrace

Far View Visitor's
Center

Far View Sites
Complex

Headquarters and
Museum Area

Cedar Tree Tower and
Farm Terraces

Mug
House

Step House

Spruce Tree House

Long
House

Badger House
Community

Soda Canyon Overlook Trail

Kodak
House

Square Tower House

Sun Temple

Cliff Palace

Fire Temple and Oak Tree House

Balcony House

Chapin Mesa Loop Road

Sun Point
Overlook

Leadville

Denver

Grand Junction

Colorado
Springs

Montrose

Salida

Telluride

Pueblo

Mancos

Durango

Alamosa

Trini

MESA VERDE
NATIONAL PARK

THE WETHERILLS
IN THE SOUTHWEST

1 - MANCOS, COLORADO
  Wetherill family Alamo Ranch, 1881-1902
2 - MESA VERDE, COLORADO
  Wetherill family guides tours 1884-1902
3 - GRAND CANYON AND HOPI VILLAGES
  Al Wetherill guides Gustaf Nordenskiöld, 1891
4 - CAVE 7, COTTONWOOD WASH, UTAH
  Wetherill discovery of Basketmakers, 1893-1894
5 - SNIDER'S WELL, COLORADO
  Richard Wetherill identifies Valley Dwellers from mass burial here, 1894
6 - HOPI VILLAGE OF WALPI
  Al and Richard guide T. Mitchell Prudden, 1895
7 - KEET SEEL, ARIZONA
  Richard Wetherill discovers site, 1895.
8 - MONTEZUMA CASTLE, ARIZONA
  Richard Wetherill excavates, 1896
9 - THOMPSON SPRINGS, UTAH
  Al Wetherill rides 200 miles to meet botanist Alice Eastwood.
  Together they collect 500 species of plants, 1896.
10 - CHACO CANYON, NEW MEXICO
  Richard and Marietta establish Pueblo Bonito trading post, 1896-1910
11 - ESCALANTE/GRAND STAIRCASE NATIONAL MONUMENT, UTAH
  Al and Clayton Wetherill lead first commercial exploration of the area, 1897
12 - MITCHELL SPRINGS, CORTEZ, COLORADO
  Clayton Wetherill excavates with T. Mitchell Prudden.
  Naming of the "Prudden Unit" of puebloan households, 1902
13 - THOREAU, NEW MEXICO
  Al Wetherill establishes trading post, 1902-1904
14 - TWO GREY HILLS, NEW MEXICO
  Winslow Wetherill establishes trading post and commissions
  first Yei Bi Chai blanket possibly by Hosteen Clah's wife, ca. 1903.
15 - CREEDE, HERMIT LAKES, COLORADO
  Home of Anna Wetherill and husband Charles Mason, 1907-1920
16 - RAINBOW BRIDGE, UTAH
  John Wetherill guides Byron Cummings and Edgar Hewett here, 1909
17 - CANYON DE CHELLEY AND CANYON DEL MUERTO, ARIZONA
  Clayton Wetherill guides here as well as to Chaco Canyon, Two Grey Hills,
  Black Lake, Sura Lee, Captain Tom Wash and Gallego Canyon, 1909
18 - KAYENTA, ARIZONA
  John Wetherill operates trading post and guide service, 1910-1945
19 - BLACK MOUNTAIN
  Winslow and Hilda Wetherill establish trading post, 1911
20 - SALANA SPRINGS
  Al and Mary Wetherill manage trading post, 1911
21 - MARSH PASS, ARIZONA
  John and Clayton Wetherill help Samuel Guernsey and A.V. Kidder from
  Harvard's Peabody Museum, 1914-1917
22 - GALLUP, NEW MEXICO
  Al Wetherill serves as postmaster, 1920s.

Thompson
Springs
9

Moab

15
Creede

Cottonwood
Canyon
4

Grand
Gulch
Hovenweep National
Monument

12 Mitchell
Springs 1 Mancos

Clay
Hill

Bluff

McElmo
Canyon 5

Mesa Verde
National Park
2

Durango

16
ow Bridge National
I Monument

The Goosenecks

Oljato

Ute Mountain
Tribal Park

Monument
Valley

Sweetwater

Keet Seel Ruins 7 18

n House Betatakin Ruin Kayenta

Farmington

Pied Valley

Ojo
Alamo

21

19 Black
Mountain

Canyon
de Chelley

14

Two Grey Hills

Hopi Villages

Sa'ana
Springs 20 17

10 Chaco Culture
National Historic Park

6 Walpi

Polacca

22 Gallup

13 Thoreau

El Morro
National
Monument

TABLE OF CONTENTS

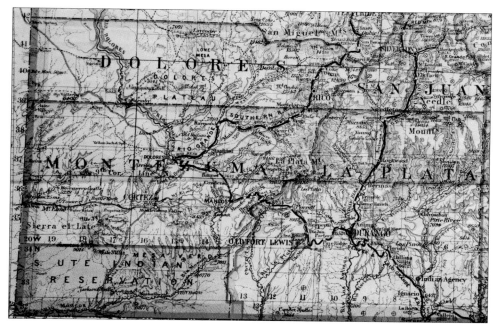

Corner of Nel's map showing Southwest Colorado in 1899

FOREWORD

There are actually two Mesa Verdes. The one most people think of is the national park containing cliff dwellings and surface ruins built by people that have come to be known as Ancestral Puebloans. The other Mesa Verde includes the park but extends well beyond that. It is a vast flat-topped land-form dressed in pinyon and juniper forests and laced by canyons.

This rugged landscape which I will call "the Mesa Verde" includes Ute Mountain Ute tribal lands as well as the Department of Interior's Mesa Verde National Park. Cliff dwellings and other ancient architectural rem-nants are scattered throughout the Mesa Verde. Any view of early explo-ration touches equally both inside and outside the boundaries of what would become the national park.

Exploration and removal of artifacts began at least as early as 1861 when prospector T. Stangl carved his name on a cliff wall above Bone Awl House. It would be 20 years before the Wetherill family would arrive and begin exploring the surroundings of their new home in the Mancos Valley. They were, in many ways, late on the scene of archaeological excavation.

My fascination with the Wetherill story began in 1974, 113 years after T. Stangl left his signature in Mancos Canyon. As a ranger for the Bureau of Land Management, I was assigned to protect cultural and natural resources on 3½ million acres of public lands administered by the Bureau of Land Management in southeastern Utah. I struggled initially, having first to re-educate myself in what that meant. Slowly and painfully, I changed my values from believing in the collection of antiquities to disapproving of removing artifacts from their original location.

Leading a mule into Grand Gulch, a 75-mile-long canyon first entered by John and Al Wetherill in 1892, I gained my initial exposure to signatures inscribed by explorers as they excavated remnants left by prehistoric people. I was a greenhorn in every sense of the word. How much I had to learn became clear when Enid the mule was nearly killed by my poor choice of travel route. Such perils aside, I was forever captured by the mystery of those early discoveries and Grand Gulch.

I viewed remnants of camps left in alcoves by intrepid explorers: tin cans, bullet casings, wooden dried apple boxes, Dutch ovens, horseshoes, and harness leather left where explorers or cowboys stored, cached, or abandoned them. Thirty-two years later, historic and prehistoric remnants have disappeared from that landscape. The artifacts that so captivated me have been hauled away by those who degrade the outdoor museum through their selfish need to possess bits and pieces of the past, leaving nothing to teach those who follow about the people who inhabited these lands centuries ago.

The Wetherill Grand Gulch Project was born in 1986, inspired by questions growing from my early wanderings as a ranger. My interest in reconnecting artifacts with long-past exploration of alcoves and cliff dwellings resulted in a four-year project by a team of unpaid volunteers. We quickly realized that graffiti left by 19th century explorers could provide connections and documentation of their activities. Our team reconnected artifacts found in museums to caves in southeastern Utah in a process I deemed "reverse archaeology." Two publications grew out of that work: *Anasazi Basketmaker, Papers from the 1990 Wetherill-Grand Gulch Symposium,* edited by Victoria Atkins, and *Cowboys and Cave Dwellers,* which I co-wrote with Ray Williamson. Historic graffiti is rapidly disappearing from the cliff walls, the victim of natural erosion and human ignorance.

Documentation of inscription graffiti improved as we developed scientific methods for recording them. My crude initial attempts evolved toward detailed maps, illustrations, and location information. Like the Wetherills, who received advice from the many visitors and scientists who worked side-by-side with them, I received help refining my techniques of analysis and documentation. In turn, those methods allowed me access to remote archaeological sites as I pieced together a history of exploration in the Four Corners.

Work in Grand Gulch, and Butler and Cottonwood washes in southern Utah was followed by documentation of signatures in 26 archaeological

Tom Wetherill, grandson of Al Wetherill, at Alamo Ranch in 1993.

sites of Ute Mountain Ute Tribal Park. That was followed by work in Mesa Verde National Park, where Larry Nordby, research archaeologist for the national park, asked for my help unraveling the long-disputed exploration of Mesa Verde National Park. I became a team member for site assessment, and our work recorded 2,300 inscriptions within just seven of the park's archaeological sites. I focused on exploration within Mesa Verde National Park prior to 1908, recording inscriptions that prompted my search for biographical information about the people who left them. I was soon knocking on doors of descendants of those who signed on walls, cliffs, or beams. Among them were descendants of the Wetherill family. I was captivated by vast amounts of early exploration history that family members had saved for generations, each of them having been told to hold onto the materials because they would some day prove important.

Tom Wetherill took the first step toward fulfilling the family's long-term desire to place these heirlooms in an archive. On his deathbed, he told his wife Wren that I should become the caretaker of Al Wetherill's collection of letters, documents, newspapers and photographs. My directive was to help the Wetherill family find an institution where researchers might utilize information held in the family files. Tom's idea quickly expanded to include the records held by numerous Wetherill relatives. The family had three choices for where to place their archives, and ultimately selected the Anasazi Heritage Center over Edge of the Cedars State

Historical Park in Blanding, Utah, and the Center of Southwest Studies at Fort Lewis College. The family, in a sense, returned documents to an institution close to the center of discoveries and beginnings of their family in the Four Corners. To date, more than 11,000 letters, photographs, newspapers, and family genealogies related to life and exploration in the Mancos Valley and Mesa Verde have been added to the collection.

My attempt to tell the Wetherill story is based upon nearly 20 years of research into Wetherill contributions to southwestern culture and archaeology. This has left me with a deep respect for the family, living as they did during a time of cultural dictates different from those of today. The changing times in which they lived involved pioneering efforts of exploration, discovery, and searches for meaning among ruins in an isolated, mystical landscape known as the Four Corners. Infighting often erupted over archaeological territories, fed by political maneuvering among scholars for "ownership" of excavations. Vehement disagreements and petty conflicts were the norm.

In the midst of that controversy, the Wetherills pursued what they considered an ordained mission to study, understand, and teach others about the people who had come before them.

– Fred M. Blackburn
Cortez, Colorado
Summer 2005

Frederick Chapin standing on the first ruin excavated by the Wetherills on Alamo Ranch, in 1889.

INTRODUCTION

The name Wetherill is closely tied to the early days of what became Mesa Verde National Park. For 20 years, the family of B.K. Wetherill explored the cliff dwellings and surface ruins along the canyons of the Mancos River drainage, guiding scientists and curiosity seekers alike. In the century since their Alamo Ranch was the center of Mesa Verde explorations, their activities among the ruins have been misunderstood, misrepresented, and harshly criticized. It is time to set the record straight.

Richard Wethereld was born in 1788 in Mulladry County, Armage, Ireland, to parents from Yorkshire, England. He arrived in New York in 1812 carrying with him a letter of greeting to the Quaker meeting house of New York.

Two years later, his name now changed to Wetherill, he married Ann Henvis, daughter of Robert and Deborah Kite Henvis. Their union produced 13 children; Benjamin Kite (B.K.) Wetherill was number 12. Unlike his siblings, B.K. chose a path westward. He is rumored to have been captured by, and/or have chosen to live with, an unidentified tribe in Wisconsin. Later, he mediated disputes on the Osage Reservation along the borders of Missouri, Kansas, and Oklahoma.

B.K. married Marian Tompkins in the small community of Rocksylvania, Iowa. Their union brought forth Alice who died in infancy, Richard, Al, Anna, John, Clayton and Winslow – all of them educated within a strict Quaker environment. Alice and Richard were born in Iowa, the rest of the children in Kansas.

In 1879 B.K. chose to seek a better life as a pioneer in Colorado. His family arrived in 1881 and shortly after – likely while building ditches and fences or clearing fields – his son John discovered an archaeological site. Their excavation of the large rubble mound in the northeast section of their property launched a lifetime pursuit for some of the Wetherill brothers. By 1882 they were exploring Ancestral Puebloan dwellings within the cliffs of southwestern Colorado's Mancos Canyon. By 1885 they were guiding others to them.

Some historians consider the Wetherill brothers ignorant cowboys. Their supporters and descendants believe the Wetherills' Quaker beliefs guided them as self-educated scholars and protectors of the archaeological treasures around them. Were they instrumental in the preservation of information and archaeological discoveries for future generations or were they pothunters, vandals interested only in the monetary rewards their collections might bring? Their excavation activities – not only at Mesa Verde but across Utah, Colorado, Arizona and New Mexico – remain controversial. Archaeologists and anthropologists often avoid a serious review of information contained in family records, denying the Wetherills credit for their role in the beginnings of southwestern archaeology.

Following the discovery of Cliff Palace in 1888, B.K. Wetherill promoted the concept of a national park years before a women's organization pushed it forward to reality in 1906. B.K. expressed his family's concern that pothunters were destroying archaeological values in many sites. Although research indicates B.K. never visited a cliff dwelling, he was familiar with archaeology from the remnants of surface structures scattered across the Mancos Valley. B.K. recognized the importance of the archaeological sites as he questioned his sons about what they were finding and what their interpretations of those finds were. He asked the Smithsonian for guidance on proper excavation techniques, but was rebuffed by an archaeologist who had done his own excavations within Mancos Canyon before the Wetherill family even arrived there.

Were Wetherill excavations appropriate for their time? Were their observations and conclusions viewed seriously by a slow-to-respond scientific community? Wetherill family notes provide insights into their discoveries. Their recorded observations may still teach us more about the Ancestral Puebloans.

Many names for southwestern archaeological sites and their localities that are now commonly used were chosen or influenced by the Wetherills, or named after them: Cliff Palace, Step House, Balcony House, Spruce Tree House, Wetherill Mesa, Keet Seel, and Betatakin are most prominent. Names they popularized for both the prehistoric architects and their architecture endure as well: Basketmaker, Prudden Unit, and Cliff Dweller.

Scholars have too often overlooked the influence of the Wetherills' Quaker beliefs on their actions. Harvey Leake, great grandson of John

Wetherill, first pointed out to me his belief that the Quaker principle of Inward Light was a primary motivation behind the Wetherills' activities.

> There was something more in the Wetherills' interest in archae-ology than respect. It was more like an obsession influenced, no doubt, by respect, but driven even more deeply by an intuition that there was significance in the "symbols of the past" (Al's termi-nology). This significance defied explanation at the time. To me, this is the essence of the Inward Light – knowing that something is right (or wrong) without fully comprehending why you feel that way.
>
> In retrospect, the Wetherills' unspoken and underlying agenda was a criticism of modern society. In short, they didn't believe that "progress" was necessarily leading us in the right direction, and felt that much could be learned from ancient societies in this regard. It was a very humanistic approach.

While individual members of the Society of Friends may interpret Inward Light in different ways, it clearly shaped the Wetherill family's sense of purpose. Leake believes that B.K.'s and his family's Quaker beliefs drove them toward an understanding of preservation and ancient culture. The Inward Light compelled the family to keep, through generations, ines-timable collections of written material and photographs. The Inward Light compelled each generation to repeat the advice: Some day these materials will be important.

One present-day Quaker, Russell Heaton, explains Inward Light this way:

> Quakers don't believe that their actions are God-directed.
> Friends believe that all people are equals. By embracing the concept of "Inward Light," they are accepting their own spirituali-ty as well as the equal spirituality of all people. Quakers also believe education is important because it leads to a fuller life. They want their feelings and beliefs respected, but are quiet persuaders rather than crusaders.

The Wetherills' Quaker beliefs led them to view whatever cultural remains they found as having been created by people who were their equals. That view made them more conscientious and inclined to treat arti-facts and structures with the same respect as they would accord one anoth-er's property.

Ray Williamson, my co-author for *Cowboys and Cave Dwellers,* stated:

> ...In the power of what Friends call the "Inward Light" ... [there is] the belief that God speaks through their inner being,

John Wetherill inscription, in Mancos Canyon within the Ute Mountain Ute Tribal Park.

when they open themselves to the light. Being open requires a form of meditation and sufficient silence to let that "Inward Light" speak to them, especially when faced with an ethical or moral dilemma.

Who were the Wetherills: cowboys, Friends, scientists, scholars, or villains? No matter what the answer, there is one undisputed certainty. The Wetherills stood apart in their attempts to record what they found, unlike countless others before, during, and after their time who excavated without making any records of what they found, removing artifacts with no concern for context. Many of those artifacts have long since disappeared into a void. Wetherill writings, as well as what others wrote about them and their findings, remain in abundance. For so many others who excavated dwellings, their only surviving documentation is the signatures they inscribed in the alcoves and on cliff dwelling walls. Whatever conclusions are drawn about the Wetherill family, they indisputably left a deep footprint upon the region known as the Four Corners.

THE WETHERILL FAMILY

Benjamin Kite Wetherill and Marian Tompkins Wetherill had seven children:
Alice, Richard, Benjamin Alfred ("Al"), Anna, John, Clayton, and Winslow.
Six of these children married and their spouses are included in this book:
Marietta Palmer, Mary Tarrant, Charles Mason, Louisa Wade,
Sisters Eugenia Faunce and Hilda Faunce and Mattie Pauline Young.

	ALICE WETHERILL 1857-1859
	RICHARD WETHERILL 1858-1910 married: **MARIETTA PALMER** 1876-1954
BENJAMIN KITE WETHERILL 1832-1898	**BENJAMIN ALFRED (AL) WETHERILL** 1861-1950 married: **MARY TARRANT** 1864-1954
son of: Richard Wetherill (1788-1869) and Ann Kite Henvis (1794 -1844) of Pennsylvania	**ANNA ISABEL WETHERILL** 1865-1937 married: **CHARLES C. MASON** 1859-1936
married: **MARIAN TOMPKINS** 1835-1923	**JOHN WETHERILL** 1866-1944 married: **LOUISA WADE** 1877-1945
daughter of: Enoch Tompkins 1782-1846 and Deborah Westbrooke 1808-1868	**CLAYTON WETHERILL** 1868-1921 married: **EUGENIA FAUNCE** 1885-1964
	WINSLOW WETHERILL **1870-1939** married: **MATTIE PAULINE YOUNG** 1875-1964 married: **HILDA FAUNCE** 1890-1979

BENJAMIN (B.K.) AND MARIAN WETHERILL

BLM Anasazi Heritage Center

B.K. Wetherill as a student

BLM Anasazi Heritage Center

Marian Tompkins Wetherill

| B | enjamin Kite (B.K.) Wetherill was the 12th child born (in 1832) to Richard Wethereld and Ann Henvis. Although Benjamin's father emigrated from Ireland, the family name was derived from a small |

area called Wetherheld in northern England, along the border of Scotland. Wetherheld is an area where wethers – castrated prepubescent male sheep – were held and protected from predators or the elements. Subsequently the name Wethereld became attached to the people who cared for the animals.

B.K. was the Wetherill family explorer, a stalwart man of balding head, small of stature and firm of belief. B.K. was well educated within the Quaker society, at Westtown Boarding School in Chester, Pennsylvania. Two of B.K.'s nephews, Richard and Robert, established a foundry and machine shop in Chester, Pennsylvania, in 1872, building Corliss engines, which had been developed in England. The enormous engines, sometimes 30 feet tall, were designed for stationary work in factories. Their foundry built, among other items, cable cars, and elevators, all of which helped ensure their financial success.

B.K. left his successful family behind for an unknown life on the frontier. He had the travel itch and purportedly lived with native tribes in the Wisconsin area before traveling south to Hardin County, Iowa. In Iowa he met and married Marian Tompkins. Their marriage in May of 1856 was the first in the community of Rocksylvania, which later was called Iowa

THE MEANING OF FRIENDS

The Religious Society of Friends grew out of a 17th century movement for religious freedom in England. In a period when various groups formed in opposition to the highly structured Church of England, founder George Fox traveled the countryside both studying and promoting a personal approach to religion, without heirarchy or dogma. He asserted that each person could gain divine guidance through his or her own "Inner Light"– also referred to as the "Inner Light of Christ" – as a child of God without any intermediary.

Fox's following grew, and called themselves Children of Light, Friends in the Truth, and eventually the Religious Society of Friends. As it remains today, a local congregation of this Christian denomination is called a "Meeting," and their gathering place a "Meeting House."

Explanations of the name Quaker vary. Fox wrote in his autobiography that when he admonished a judge to "tremble at the word of the Lord," the judge responded by calling him a "quaker." Other versions of the story claim a judge warned someone to "quake" before God. Although the term was considered derogatory for many years, it has generally become accepted by Friends, to the point that both terms are in common use today.

Often described as pacifists, members of the Religious Society of Friends more accurately believe in a peaceful response to all forms of injustice, rather than violence or acquiescence. Their belief in the equality of all people also led Friends to adopt simple attire and speech. Rather than using "you," which carried with it implications of social class, they addressed one another as "thee" and "thou." Similarly, they used only plain buttons and wore no collars, because such things "of means" were deemed unnecessary.

Falls. B.K. was 24 years old. Marian, and possibly B.K., may have been involved in the Underground Railroad abolition movement during the 1850s, as many members of their community were. Her ancestors included Daniel D. Tompkins, vice president of the United States from 1817 to 1825 under President James Monroe.

After the birth of their son Richard, the young couple traveled west toward the Missouri River, carrying with them the well wishes of the Friends in their Iowa Quaker community. B.K. ran a grocery store in Leavenworth, Kansas, where they settled in 1859. He moved his family to Diamond Island on the Missouri River sometime around 1864, but flooding forced them to return to Leavenworth in 1867.

Building on his earlier experiences in Wisconsin, B.K. moved to the Osage reservation in 1872 at the age of 40, leaving his family in Leavenworth. Quakers had been known to work well with Native Americans since the signing of the William Penn treaties in 1682. When former indigenous territories were further and further diminished to become Indian reservations after the Civil War, Quaker leaders persuaded Ulysses S. Grant to use their mediation skills to help with native resettlement. Appointed Indian Agent for the Osage as a result of these directives, B.K. worked with the Osage, Wichita, and other tribes until 1876. During that time he mediated multiple intertribal disputes along the Oklahoma-Missouri border, as well as conflicts between cattle drivers and the tribes they encountered in the region.

In 1876, B.K. left the Osage reservation and settled his family in Joplin, Missouri. There he and his elder sons Richard and Al (now 16 and 15) worked in lead mining. It proved devastating to B.K., who suffered lifelong poisoning from breathing white lead dust and fumes generated by lead processing. Prospects low and health suffering, he once again pointed his horse west.

BLM Anasazi Heritage Center

B.K. around the time he worked on the Osage Reservation.

America had changed quickly after the Civil War, particularly the northern industrial states, which benefited from the war. Rails reached west competing for arrival on the Pacific Coast, as well as building a network of lines to haul vast riches from mines in the Rocky Mountains and cattle from the plains. Where there had been only covered wagons or packhorses for transportation, rails and the Iron Horse now provided a means for reaching new areas. Settlement in new, uncharted country offered a means for displaced Union and Confederate veterans to begin again, and many settled in the Montezuma and Mancos valleys of Colorado.

Leaving his family behind, B.K. accompanied acquaintances from the Missouri lead mines, relatives of a family named Mitchell who settled in the Montezuma Valley. B.K. took up the life of a prospector while looking carefully at all options for relocating his family to southwestern Colorado. Contrary to some versions of his family's history, he did not settle his family along the San Juan River (where he staked claims for himself and his sons), but initially chose to be near the mines in Rico. Miss Minnie Rush, of Dolores, recorded that three men, James Martin Rush, John J. Wade (grandfather and father, respectively, of Louisa Wade Wetherill), and B.K. Wetherill, left mining and the mountains of Rico to "bach" together in the

B.K., Marian and Alice Wetherill.

Lawrence, Kansas, 10 Mo 26 1875 —

Dear Wife —

Arrive here all right last night might just as well stayed at home as the harness are already shipped — Chase went to Leavenworth this morning. I did not see him but understand he will telegraph to Jesse to wait at Coffeyville one day for him. They are having some trouble at the Agency in regard to rations. Chase has gone to the fort for Soldiers. Say nothing about this to any one — as it may all blow over. Love to all —

Thy Loving

B.K.

Letter from B.K. to Marian.

BLM Anasazi Heritage Center

Train trestle and water tower at Hesperus, ca. 1897.

Mancos Valley. The three men liked the valley and agreed to settle there. B.K. saw potential for agriculture, or as Al so eloquently stated, "a back to the soil epidemic struck them in the spring." B.K. leased some farm land in the Mancos Valley with thoughts of raising crops for the nearby booming mining town of Rico.

B.K. wanted to bring Marian and their six children to the Mancos River Valley. He asked Richard to join him in 1880, to help establish a homestead capable of housing the rest of the family. Richard arrived in late 1879 or early 1880, followed in 1881 by the rest of the family. The burden of preparation for their arrival was placed upon Richard and B.K. Al Wetherill recorded the family journey, stating that since Wetherill brothers worked for the railroad they only had to choose the route and the railroad as the family all received passes for the journey. But the Denver & Rio

A very early family photograph of the Alamo Ranch.

Grande Railroad extended only as far as Alamosa, Colorado, nearly 300 miles from their destination of Mancos. They crossed the Continental Divide, likely near Cumbres Pass, before reaching Mancos. It would be many years before travelers could take the more direct route over what became known as Wolf Creek Pass. B.K. met his family at the Alamosa railhead, helping them complete the final trek to Mancos. Al noted the joy all the children experienced while on the trail:

> The trip was a near-heavenly journey for the kids and they had to be corralled at night to keep them from wandering out of the camp grounds when they should have been sleeping. The children were always wide awake to the new and strange surroundings that were met up with and passed each day. The wonderful clear skies at night showed the stars so much closer than they had ever been seen from the thick atmosphere of the Missouri bottomlands. Father's long trek to Alamosa and back set the agricultural deal a hard blow for awhile...

They settled on glacially worn alluvial flow, drawing on their Pennsylvania experience and Quaker persistence to create fields, gardens,

A JOURNEY BROUGHT TO LIFE

The journal of a Mancos visitor, Leander F. Hayes, brings life to the arduous trip from Missouri to Mancos. Leander journeyed to Mancos 12 years after the Wetherill family, hoping the western climate would slow or cure his tuberculosis. His brother William Henry Hayes had settled in Mancos in 1878, built the first school there with Andrew Menefee, and by 1880 was a Justice of the Peace. In 1884, William Henry had accompanied S.E. Osborn and George W. Jones in their exploration for coal within the Mesa Verde, during which they excavated a number of cliff dwellings.

> On the morning of October 3rd 1893. We, Ma & Myself took passage on the Santifee Train, for a trip for my health, from our home in St. Joseph Mo, to Mancos, Colorado. Via. Topeka Kansas. – Pueblo-Salida and Durango Colorado. We spent half a day in Pueblo. One night in Salida. Thurs. a.m. Oct 5th we once are again on our way. on the D&R.G. Narrow Gague R.R. Oh what a change from the grand and commodious sleeper, to the dirty cramped (unreadable) narrow gague coaches. However, they appeared much better when I became accustomed to it. From here we began to ascend the mountains. frost and light snow are all about us.
>
> I noticed the passengers kept their overcoats on. Women their heavy cloaks. while I was rather warm. I took my overcoat off, opened my coat and vest, and stood on the platform outside. Oh how I did enjoy that cold, bracing, pure mountain air …
>
> It gets dark here so quick. Soon can see nothing outside, lamps are lighted. I am very weary.
>
> It was 9:15 P.M. when we arrived at Durango. We stoped at the Blair House. Oct. 6th. Here we again change cars to the D.&R.G. Southern … This is quite a new road, and so many short curves. This morning we are in great coal fields. 40 miles of country near Durango …
>
> At 11 AM we arived in Mancos and found all well. Bro. Wm Henry was thrashing wheat.

outbuildings, and home. B.K. understood it would require his entire family's efforts to survive in this recently settled outpost of the American West.

A large, fallen Ancestral Puebloan site was located on the northeastern portion of their homestead and remains there to this day. At this cobble pueblo they had their first encounter with cultural remnants of the people who had occupied this land hundreds of years before them. But in those first years, Wetherill family labors focused on construction of the homestead, leaving little free time for exploration of the "Aztecs," a local term coined during that era to describe those long-vanished people. The family's persistent hard work yielded a sturdy home and outbuildings, including work-shops and an ice house, and irrigation ditches lined by parallel rows of cotton-wood trees. In future years ranch guests would find the tree-lined ditches a delightfully cool place to swing in hammocks while reading books from the family's extensive library. For now, the trees inspired the name for the ranch: Alamo, Spanish for poplar, the family of trees that includes cottonwoods.

Hay was stored in a barn they built without a nail, using lap and tongue-in-groove joints held together by hard oak pegs driven in augured holes. A testa-ment to their construction skills, the barn still stands on the property today. B.K. and his sons combined homesteads, adjoining them where possible. Homestead claims by adult family members were needed to create a combined total of land sufficient for the family's survival. Through homesteading and pur-chases, B.K. and his sons accumulated at least 600 acres by 1898. According to newspaper editor W.H. "Muldoon" Kelly, they were farming nearly 1,000 acres by 1893, much of it possibly leased by the Wetherill family. They employed many laborers – including Charlie Mason who was newly married to daughter Anna – drawing from a pool of people available in the Mancos Valley. B.K.'s business sense was keen as the family's holdings grew. They commonly used sev-eral draft teams for plowing and harvesting as they expanded their ranch. The older Wetherill brothers hired out as packers and freighters for the numerous mines dotting the face of the La Plata Mountains.

B.K. and his sons quickly cultivated relationships with local Ute, migra-tory Pueblo, and later Navajo people during the 1880s. The Brunot Agreement, implemented in 1873, preserved hunting rights for the Utes, while curtailing their summer migrations into the Shining Mountains (now known as the La Plata and San Juan mountains). Centuries of tradi-tion and migration had been removed with a single pen stroke. Utes were blamed for theft, and in many cases shot on sight, leaving little incentive for interaction with local miners, cowboys, or settlers. Utes adapted tradi-tions such as the Bear Dance – usually held upon their arrival to the high mountain pastures as bears awoke in their dens – to other locations farther west in order to avoid interactions with paranoid miners and cowboys.

The Wetherills' skills of mediation, firm tolerance and acceptance soon marked the family ranch as a refuge for the afflicted as well as a favorite place for social events. Marian, B.K., and their family never left the needy unattended.

Despite his deteriorating health, B.K. and Marian set the example for their family as to the treatment of all people, the importance of education, and their Quaker belief that all relationships should be peaceful, including those with the Utes. Drawing on his experiences with the tribes associated with the Osage, B.K. negotiated with the Ute people for the right to graze his family's livestock in Indian Territory along the Mancos River, securing those rights in the midst of a very hostile land grab by settlers and cowboys from displaced Utes. The firm understanding he established with the Ute people allowed his family to be in the place where they sighted legendary Cliff Palace. They read,

THE UTES AND THE WESTERN SLOPE

Under Chief Ouray's skilled leadership, and because of the belligerence of Chief Colorow, the Utes managed to keep white settlement out of western Colorado through a series of treaties and friendships with whites including Kit Carson and John Wesley Powell. When prospectors discovered gold in Colorado in 1858, hordes of miners poured into Ute territory so the federal government requested a treaty designating reservation boundaries. In the treaty of 1868 the Utes received title to one-third of Colorado territory and the right to bar any whites from entering the Western Slope and the peaks they called "The Shining Mountains." At the height of his diplomatic powers, Chief Ouray had negotiated a generous treaty, which he insisted be made "final forever."

As late as the 1870s Colorado remained a frontier, and the carefully negotiated Treaty of 1868 provided the Utes with more than 16 million acres on Colorado's Western Slope. Considering that the Utes probably never exceeded 4,000 to 5,000 people, their defense of their mountain homeland against other Indian tribes and white incursions was remarkable.

But white settlers continued to encroach on Ute lands, and prospectors discovered gold in the rugged San Juan Mountains of Southwest Colorado. Six years after the treaty guaranteeing the Utes one-third of Colorado, Chief Ouray and others signed the Brunot Agreement in which Utes gave up the mineral-rich San Juans. Ute Indian trails would provide access for the first organized expedition of American scientists into the Colorado Rockies later that year,

BLM Anasazi Heritage Center

Ute families in Mancos Canyon ca. 1898.
This photograph was taken by Sumner Matheson.

Ute family in Mancos Canyon ca. 1874. This is likely a photo taken by William Henry Jackson.

when teams of geographers and geologists working with F.V. Hayden began to map the territory of Colorado. The surveys continued for three seasons, representing some of the most remarkable work ever done in the United States with a sextant and transit, triangulating straight survey lines off the highest peaks and drawing into the final report - published in Washington in 1879 – canyons, creeks, and alluvial fans with remarkable scale and detail.

In 1879, Ute warriors pinned down Buffalo Soldiers in Northwest Colorado at Milk Creek after angry Utes killed Agent Nathan Meeker because he had withheld their food and promised annuities. Chief Ouray tried to defuse the Meeker situation, but whites in Denver would have nothing short of the complete removal of the Utes. An entire nation would be forced off their ancestral lands because of the depradations of a few. By 1880 a hastily written treaty in Washington, D.C., forced the White River Utes onto the Uintah Indian Reservation in northeastern Utah. Other bands, now known as the Southern Utes and Ute Mountain Utes, were forced onto a reservation south and west of Durango.

On September 4, 1881, the General Land Office threw open Ute reservation lands in western Colorado to settlement. That same year, B.K. Wetherill's family journeyed west to join him in building a family homestead in the Mancos Valley.

— Andrew Gulliford

Frederick Chapin photographed these Ute men with Richard Wetherill at Alamo Ranch in 1889.

studied, and followed the 1878 publication of the *Hayden Surveys into Southwest Colorado specifically the report on Ancient Ruins of S.W. Colorado, examined during the summers of 1875 and 1876* by William H. Holmes and *Ruins of S.W. Colorado in 1875 and 1877* by William Henry Jackson, initially following them much as a road map to discovery. They pored over the information in an attempt to identify locations and any archaeological information provided by the early reports. A much worn, musty, tattered copy remains in the possession of Richard Wetherill's descendants.

The Wetherills' relationship with Utes was not at all typical of the times, or of others who explored ruins within reservation boundaries. Leander Hayes described an encounter as he and several companions traveled through Mancos Canyon in 1893. First a solitary Ute rode toward them on horseback at high speed, stopped suddenly, stared at them and then rode away. Soon thereafter, they encountered two Utes.

> We tried to Chow Wow with them but failed totally. We started on. They allso started. We one way. They the other. Mary and Nellie had become quite nervous. It was now dark but, The moon shone brightly above us.
>
> Shortly, our Guide who was in the advance, said to the one next him, hurry up, and pass the word back, hurry up. Soon the word reached me. I was in the rear. Each one whispered to the one next behind him. We pressed forward fast as our little loaded buros could trot with their packs. We behind could not determine what was the occasion. We were in the narrow canon now.

The group hastened up a steep, narrow trail, hearing noises they believed were Indians. Once over the mountain, the guide acknowledged there were Indians driving horses on the other side of the river. Assured by the guide that they were now safe, the group made camp for the night even though they were still on the reservation. It probably was not a restful night.

> We made our beds among the quaking asps so as to be hid from the light of the fire and retired. Two years before this the Ute Indians killed a white man near, if not, right here. He ventured here alone.

B.K. firmly believed that discovery and excavation of archaeological sites by many visitors and locals would inevitably lead to their destruction. His beliefs were so strong that in 1889, shortly after a party led by Charles McLoyd excavated in Cliff Palace, Spruce Tree House, and Square Tower House, B.K. wrote a letter to the United States National Museum, a division of the Smithsonian.

> We are particular to preserve the buildings, but fear, unless the Govt. sees proper to make a national park of the Canons, including Mesa Verde, the tourists will destroy them...
> I would like for the party to work under the auspices of your institution. As I expect them to make a thorough search, and get many interesting relics, particularly from a number of cliff houses. Discovered by my son R. Wetherill, during the past summer, while guiding touists over the mountains to view the dwellings.

B.K.'s letter also asked for guidance on proper methods of excavation and included notes from his son Richard's journal as an example of their current methods of excavation. It reached Smithsonian Secretary S.P. Langley, who forwarded the correspondence to John Wesley Powell at the Bureau of Ethnology. Powell in turn passed it on to archaeologist William H. Holmes who answered the inquiry after an extensive delay. Curator of Collections for the Smithsonian, Holmes knew the archaeological resources of the area since he had excavated a small collection from Mancos Canyon while on the Hayden Survey in 1875. That collection already resided in the Smithsonian. (It is unclear what became of another early collection which Lewis H. Morgan purchased in 1878 from General Heffernan, of Animas City.) Although Langley was inclined to accept artifacts from the Wetherills, Holmes successfully argued that any artifacts for the Smithsonian should come from his own explorations in the area.

Not only did Holmes reject artifacts from the Wetherills because he wanted to do his own collecting, but he also rejected B.K.'s request for guidance on proper scientific methods. He essentially told B.K. that he was incapable of following them.

...Of course I would be very much pleased if as you suggest we could in some way direct the work laid out by you, but it does not seem practicable at present to do so. For scientific purposes at least one half of the value of collections depend upon the record of data relating to place and manner of discovery. If your people were required to keep and capable of keeping such records there would be less need of scientific supervision...

Having written the letter to B.K., Holmes sent an interoffice memo to Langley.

...Respectfully returned to H.W.H. the matters referred to within are of as much interest to me personally that I have taken the liberty of writing directly to Mr. Wetherill. There seems to be no need of other communication with him...

Langley wrote B.K. in February of 1890, obviously frustrated by the stone wall built by Holmes. Although Holmes wanted to do his own collecting in order to control the excavations, Langley was disappointed that he would not obtain the Wetherills' collection for the Smithsonian. It is important to note that Langley, in his capacity as Secretary of the Smithsonian, encouraged the Wetherills to continue collecting artifacts and wished them well in selling them.

I regret that, as I told you in my letter of January 22, the Smithsonian Institution unfortunately is unable to make arrangements for obtaining large collections of this kind, but hope that your sons will have no difficulty in disposing advantageously of their collections.

Holmes' own territorial interests for obtaining control of collection and excavation in the drainages of the Mancos River outweighed any possibility of encouraging the Wetherills, no matter how honest their appeal for help.

In 1875, Holmes had excavated a site in lower Mancos Canyon currently known as Sixteen Window House. He subsequently wrote about his expectations – and concerns – for discovery of artifacts within Mancos Canyon following this, his initial exploration of what he believed to be Aztec sites. Archaeological exploration was often driven during the time period by earlier rumors that had begun in the 16th century, of cities of gold. Fostered by the Pueblo people of the Rio Grande to rid their villages of Spanish intruders, the rumors persisted into the 19th century, promising riches to be found within cities farther north. Holmes' comments in his journal from 1875 suggest he was at least mindful of such rumors.

William H. Jackson photograph of Sixteen Window House ca. 1889.

B.K., Anna Wetherill Mason and Marian at Alamo Ranch in 1891.

They are gone now indeed and have been for centuries and now like vandals we invade their homes and sack their cities. We at least, carry off the earthen jars in triumph and reprimand them for not having left us more gold and jewels.

Thwarted in their quest for help from the experts at the Smithsonian, B.K. and his family turned to others who might be able to teach them how to follow scientific methods in their excavations.

What might we have learned as a society about the archaeology of the Mesa Verde if Holmes had responded differently to the Wetherills' appeal for help? If he had chosen instead a path of education and advisement, involving the Wetherill family in documentation, the records of early excavations would have been preserved. The information that was lost because of his territoriality – including Richard Wetherill's field notes – is irreplaceable.

B.K. maintained hands-on control of family finances and correspondence until kidney failure induced by lead poisoning incapacitated him. As his health declined, his eldest son Richard was forced to assume increased responsibilities for the ranch. B.K.'s daughter Anna worked hard to maintain the household as caretaker for her father, hostess, housekeeper, and cook. Marian provided a firm set of expectations regarding operation and standards for the household.

B.K. Wetherill

Marian Wetherill

She stayed focused upon her children's education, serving as instructor to both their religious and academic knowledge. Marian was always especially pleased to receive a book that could be added to the growing family library.

B.K.'s death in 1898 at the age of 66 changed life at the Alamo Ranch. Marian, at times ailing herself, traveled among family, eventually settling with daughter Anna and her husband Charlie Mason at Hermit Lakes near Creede, Colorado. John's wife Louisa found her taxing at times, so the job of caretaking once again fell on daughter Anna. Marian died in 1923 at Rignall, Washington, having accompanied Charlie and Anna to their new home there. Responsibility for the ranch fell squarely on the shoulders of Al Wetherill after 1898. Two years earlier, Richard Wetherill and his new bride Marietta had settled at their Pueblo Bonito homestead, Richard's major undertaking in Chaco Canyon, New Mexico. B.K. and Marian had witnessed within their lifetime a growing national interest in Mesa Verde archaeology. The high standards and expectations he established provided a solid foundation that would guide sons, daughter, and their families' lives and pursuits long after his death.

RICHARD WETHERILL

A RUINS MAN

R ichard Wetherill, eldest surviving child of B.K. and Marian, was born in Hardin County, Iowa, in 1858. He held his role as eldest son in a Quaker family close to his heart, a responsibility he felt and met at all points in his life. Well educated by his parents, Richard had little time before his death at 52 to reflect or to write about his life's work. But his notes that survive and the stories about him in other family members' writings represent a man of great intellectual curiosity and keen analytical thinking.

Frank McNitt, in *Richard Wetherill: Anasazi*, suggested that writing was not Richard's strong suit, a characterization that has shaped historic opinion of him.

Richard Wetherill, 1904, St. Louis.

When he gripped a pen, however, the wells of expression dried up and his style resolved into awkward sentences.

The evidence actually suggests that Richard Wetherill was anything but an ignorant cowboy. His notes are clearly written and to the point, with strong evidence of forethought in the formation of word, sentence, and paragraph. Richard had learned Quaker traits of consensus, mediation, and adherence to the Inward Light. Craving knowledge and surrounded by the growing library in his parent's home, he read classics and science of the period. He could be stern when unfairness crossed his bow, but exuded a quiet, powerful air of respect toward others. He was not a man to be bent easily, and he devoted his life to the study of Ancestral Puebloan cultural remains. That passion and drive earned him the nickname "Ruins Man."

Richard was a true researcher. He delved deeply into subjects that interested him, inquired thoroughly in the written word, and incorporated what he learned into his conclusions. He was a pioneer in both the physical and intellectual sense. He and his brothers recognized common characteristics that suggested a relationship between existing Puebloan people and the long-gone architects of the Mesa Verde. Many of his observations are yet to be explored as valuable research themes.

Richard's conclusion that the Basketmaker culture was a predecessor to the Cliff Dweller was thought by many noted archaeologists of the time to be the notion of a charlatan. They believed he created the idea of a precursor culture to stimulate interest in artifacts and increase his sales. But eight years after his untimely death in Chaco Canyon, his theory was proven correct. Excavating cultural remnants of the Basketmaker people within caves found in Marsh Pass, Arizona, archaeologists Alfred Vincent Kidder and Samuel Guernsey recognized similarities to Richard's reports from Cottonwood Wash and Grand Gulch. Assimilating his information into their own observations, they provided Richard posthumous credit for his theories and discoveries. Kidder wrote about the Wetherill brothers' contributions to Southwest archaeology in a 1935 article in *American Anthropologist.*

> When Guernsey began his field work in the Southwest, almost nothing was known regarding the origins of Pueblo culture. The Wetherill brothers had, it is true, unearthed remains in southeastern Utah, which they believed to be different from, and older than, those of the Cliff-dwellers. But their findings, published in summary form by Prudden and Pepper, were looked upon with some skepticism. Nor had any serious attempt been made by other students to check their results and to determine whether or not there was genetic relationship between Basket Maker and Pueblo.
>
> In 1914, during his first expedition to Arizona, Guernsey discovered Basket Maker burials in Monument Valley. His study of the accompanying specimens convinced him of the authenticity of the Wetherills' materials...

Richard stands apart from his brothers by virtue of his drive to more deeply understand the Ancestral Puebloans. His curiosity drove him to search into the recesses of the Southwest for answers. Each new displaced broken bit of knowledge added to the last until he could assemble the fractured pieces into a whole vessel.

Richard and B.K. maintained a close relationship and mutual respect. The father's deep love for his eldest son is evident in the last two lines of his letter sent from Mancos in 1879, in which he asked his 19-year-old son to help him establish a new home for the family.

> What kind of work does thee do for M&S – don't expose thyself to white-lead fumes at any price. My health has improved. Ever since I left Joplin am getting right stout. Write me a good long letter, be a good boy and avoid all evil associations.

Richard was working as a mechanic for the railroad in Atchison, Kansas,

Letter from B.K. to Richard.

at the time. He quit his job and organized basic materials needed to establish the Mancos Valley homestead. B.K. advised Richard on what to bring.

> In regard to tools, etc., I would not try to bring anything except what thee wants to use in case thee got a mechanical job – farming tools can be bought at end of R.R. cheaper than hauling them through & and after you get here and we get through Summer work, will have to go there for winter supplies. Besides we would not have much use for them next summer. The true policy will be to get a team, clothes for Mother and children & Ida, grub, a small Sheet Iron Stove (Shovel & pick will need on road. Ax etc.) & save all the money you can & out of what I raise, & work we will be able to do. I think we can weather it through nobly. It is terribly lonely here without you & my feeling is for you all to come at once as if you don't one of us will have to go back. I have about ten acres plowed.

Once the family arrived, the work of preparing the land, building fences, digging an irrigation ditch and removing glacially rounded rock to make the fields tillable proved all-consuming. B.K., Richard, and Al worked every angle for income to pay for buying land and making improvements. Brothers John, Clayton, and Win were young, not yet fully capable of manhood responsibilities.

**The Wetherill brothers photographed by Frederick Chapin.
From left: Al, John, Richard (seated) and Clayton. Winslow is missing.**

A Frederick Chapin photograph of Richard Wetherill in First Ruin (Sandal House) 1889.

An agreement with the Utes allowed the Wetherills to graze cattle on their lands along the river and up the numerous side canyon tributaries of the Mancos River. Sometime in 1882 Richard made his first trek to a cliff dwelling, venturing down the river. He likely followed the adventurous steps of Al, reaching First Ruin, which had been named prior to the Wetherills' arrival. A protected, multi-roomed structure that was well hidden in an alcove above the streambed, this archaeological site is the first cliff dwelling viewed when entering the Mancos Canyon and following the river's downstream course. Richard left a rare signature and date on the ruin, small and delicately penciled on a pecked stone slab in the dwelling. Richard later changed the name of First Ruin to Sandal House, after the family's excavations in 1889 and 1890 uncovered a copious number of sandals.

By 1885 Al, Richard, and John guided the willing and the hearty deep into the dark, pinyon pine recesses of upper Mancos Canyon. Respected for their knowledge, honesty, and solid demeanor, they were soon in demand. With no roads, they had to follow travois paths left by migrating Utes, traces etched into the dark Mancos shale riverbanks and hillsides.

Not all settlers in the area enjoyed good relations with the Utes, nor did the other tribes that periodically came into the area. The Fort Lewis military post located east of the Wetherill ranch along the La Plata River was ordered to monitor such conflicts from 1880 to 1891. Originally established with one troop, including a few Buffalo Soldiers, in Pagosa Springs in 1878, Fort Lewis moved to the La Plata River in 1880 to be closer to the Ute reservation allotments. Some military personnel sought the Wetherill family's advice and guidance when entering Mancos Canyon.

LADY EXCAVATORS

Captain Baker was not alone. Military inscriptions are found in cliff dwellings throughout Mancos Canyon, indicating that army personnel – and their spouses and friends – frequently collected artifacts from ancient sites. One description of such activities was written by Bernard James Byrne, a U.S. Army surgeon.

BLM Anasazi Heritage Center

A wrapped Helen Sumner, center, prepares to ride. She was allergic to the sun.

The attractive wife of Judge Sumner, judge of the court at Durango formed quite an attachment to Laura [wife of Surgeon Byrne]. Both became experts in locating Indian graves; they would return from a day's journey with beautiful specimens of pottery, plaques, cups and pitchers, some richly decorated.

"You wouldn't believe what hard work it is," admitted Mrs. Sumner. "Sometimes we dig two to five feet in the hard ground and get nothing. But when we discover a beautiful pitcher or vase, we get such a thrill!"

As the two were preparing one morning to start on one of these explorations in Mrs. Sumner's buckboard, Nance suddenly appeared. He had with him a frail-looking but pretty young woman whom he introduced as Mrs. Nance. Mrs. Sumner invited her to join them. She accepted the invitation with evident pleasure. They did not return till dark, Laura saying they had a hard day's work but had found some beautiful pottery. Nance was waiting for them with what patience he could muster. He and his wife left at once, promising to come again.

"She was the most superstitious little thing," Mrs. Sumner said later. "When she fully realized we were intent on opening graves she nearly fainted, said no relics could pay her for such desecration, and, when we laughed at her, declared she knew Indian ghosts would haunt her the rest of her life. She sat on the ground near us but not near enough to see into the graves."

A Frontier Army Surgeon, Life in Colorado in the Eighties,
by Bernard James Byrne, M.D., Surgeon, United States Army

Captain Stephen Baker, guided by Richard or Al, arrived in 1883. Baker chose to excavate a site, presumably with troops, sometime during or after this initial exploration.

Richard guided "Surgeon" Comfort into the canyon in 1885. Comfort represented Fort Lewis military personnel in an attempt to better under-

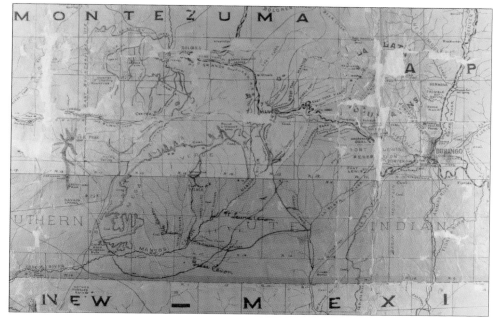

An 1893 map that belonged to Al Wetherill. His notes are visible.

stand the lay of the land, and likely had heard stories from the adventurous Captain Baker about his excavations a year or two earlier. Al, who was encamped in a Ute wickiup while monitoring cattle near the mouth of Soda Canyon, joined them for a brief time, but chose to walk farther into Soda Canyon in search of archaeological sites reported by the S.E. Osborn party and/or T.W. Wattles the year before. Richard and Dr. Comfort turned south, possibly crossing a basalt volcanic intrusion Richard called the "blowout," then riding south and east towards Acowitz Canyon. Along the way, they named many of the side canyons along Mancos Canyon.

Meanwhile back at the Alamo Ranch, Richard and his brothers wore out the pages and binding reading the 1879 Hayden survey report as they rediscovered prehistoric dwellings described by Ernest Ingersoll and W.H. Holmes. They studied in detail photographs taken by William Henry Jackson on 1874 and 1875 expeditions through the canyon. Excavating the Brownstone Front (Hemenway House 2) heightened the Wetherills' interest in expanding their own knowledge. Agreements reached with the Utes allowed them access to rougher side canyons. In time, they learned so much about the area that they explored well beyond the photographs and writings of Jackson, Holmes, and Ingersoll.

Many people explored and excavated sites in Mancos Canyon before and after the Wetherills, but most of them approached excavation and collection of relics as a novelty. One such expedition was reported by the

Durango Idea newspaper (circa 1890) as leaving for La Boca, in New Mexico, to dig up "Aztecs." This large group of men organized 30 horses into a military formation complete with major, captain, and several lieutenants.

> A caravan of 30 horses and 15 burros was required to transport the "explorers" and the following necessities to military life: 5 cases of chewing tobacco, 3 cases of beer, 10 gallons of heavy liquids, 4 burro-loads of the stuff that busted Parliament, 7 reels of fuse, a box of soap, 2 boxes of cigars, a fish line, 20 pairs of rubber boots, 200 loaves of bread, a can of lard, and one pound of bacon. The editor noted that Ranchmen should beware. These folks are bad after chickens and other ranch truck.

The Wetherills continued the hard work of ranch life while expanding their cattle herd. Winter feed was required to maintain animals during cold, snowy months. Located along the Mancos River in a valley below the La Plata Mountains, their ranch was subject to severe winter weather as cold air drained across their fields from the high peaks. Farming was an integral part of the operation, demanding summer attention. Plowing fields, cleaning ditches, cutting, drying, and stacking hay, and threshing grain were constant demands on their time from April until September. Other than feeding livestock, winter months provided a respite from summer's grueling agricultural routines and allowed time for exploration.

During the winter of 1888, Richard and brother-in-law Charlie Mason would make the discovery of a lifetime leading to a lifetime of discovery. Acowitz, ancestor of the present-day House family from the Ute Mountain Ute Tribe, reportedly told Richard of a large city located somewhere deep in the head of a canyon. Yet it would be missing cattle that led to Richard and Charlie's discovery. Whether they ever found and returned the cattle was lost to the moment.

Marietta Wetherill, whom Richard married in 1896, eight years after the discovery, reported years later that Acowitz came to the Alamo Ranch to inform Richard about tracks – believed to be from Wetherill family cattle – leading onto the mesa. According to Marietta, in a most descriptive and believable account, Acowitz returned to the location with Charlie Mason and Richard in tow. Following the cattle's hoof prints in snow and mud, the three men switchbacked upward through black clay shale beds following a long-used Ute trail. Reaching the cliff ledge, they climbed through a crack in the whitened sandstone mesa rim, then followed a crude rock trail to reach the heavily forested mesa. They tracked meandering, grazing cattle through a tangled mass of short pinyon and juniper, eventually reaching a point where they either found the cattle, took a rest, or spotted a most impressive sight. In 1950, Marietta recounted in oral histories conducted by Louis Blachly what she was told of that day: Richard spied Cliff Palace only after Acowitz tapped him on the shoulder and said, "Come see big city."

Richard and Charlie climbed into the site they named Cliff Palace over bald sandstone slick rock, utilizing downed timber and lassos with which they made temporary ladders. Arriving at their destination intact, they made a cursory inspection and left, taking with them many mental notes but less than half a dozen artifacts. They returned to their horses, exploring further by horseback around canyon heads to also view for the first time Spruce Tree House and Square Tower House. Their journey left little time for excavation or exploration within the alcoves. Writing in *The Professor's House*, Willa Cather forever embedded in the imagination of the American public a view of Cliff Palace through snowflakes. The assumption behind her romantic description was author's license though; Wetherill accounts tell nothing of a snowstorm.

Fred Blackburn Collection/Gustaf Nordenskiöld

Richard and family friend Acowitz at Alamo Ranch in 1891.

ACOWITZ, A FRIEND

Acowitz Canyon was named by the Wetherills in honor of their Ute friend and confidante. It is now known as Johnson Canyon, and was likely renamed after S.W. Johnson, who was one of the first Mancos cowboys to winter cattle within Mancos Canyon prior to increasing tensions with the Utes. Johnson inscribed a January 27, 1880, date within Sixteen Window House.

Retracing their steps, Richard and Charlie left the mesa, perhaps driving cattle through the rim crack, and down clay beds, safely reaching the canyon bottom 700 feet below. They then turned their tough ranch horses upstream along the Mancos River, past the alkaline-whitened mouth of Soda Canyon, following a trail through deep green sagebrush while viewing Two Story Ruin, sheltered high on the southern canyon wall.

Eventually they reached "Maple Camp," a long-established comfortable stopping place close to the Mancos River, used by Indians, ranchers, and explorers alike. The branches of multiple box elder trees served as a shading umbrella during summer months. Closely related to the maple, the box elders were a natural marker for the mouth of Moccasin Canyon. It is like-

Fred Blackburn Collection/Courtesy of Emerald Flint Patrick

Wash Patrick and coyote hides, ca 1890.

ly that here at Maple Camp, Richard and Charlie met Wash Patrick, Charles McLoyd, and J.H. Graham, a group of men excavating archaeological sites while also attempting to trap along the Mancos River. Charlie and Richard knew the men, whom Charlie referred to as "friends," and they freely discussed their incredible discovery. McLoyd was leader of the group whose excavations were financed in part by Jack Parsons, a Durango druggist with an interest in curios.

After a brief stop, Charlie and Richard continued on, eager to share news of their discovery with family back at the Alamo Ranch. They agreed that John would return to Maple Camp to join McLoyd's party in the excavation of Cliff Palace. At that point they were unconcerned about sharing their discovery with the McLoyd party. But McLoyd quickly realized the importance of Richard and Charlie's discovery. The four men left horses, likely turning them loose to fend for themselves, while storing their belongings at the camp or in nearby cliffs so they could travel light. Leaving the horses behind allowed them to travel through rugged terrain and give full attention to excavation without worrying about caring for animals. Rucksacks on their backs replaced their packhorse. Walking down Mancos Canyon with McLoyd in charge, they retraced Charlie and Richard's steps up through the clay and white rim, eventually making their way to Cliff Palace. Contrary to popular belief, Richard played no further part in the first known excavation of Cliff Palace. Charlie Mason helped to pack in food and carry artifacts out to the ranch.

Charles McLoyd completed his initial excavations by spring of 1889, taking artifacts to Denver where they were eventually sold for $3,000 to

From left: Wash Patrick, Jack Parsons and Lloyd Huntsman ca. 1900.

the Colorado Historical Society. Charles McLoyd paid his men a portion of the profits on June 29, 1889: $500 each to J.H. Graham and L.C. Patrick, $475 to John Wetherill, and $225 to Charlie Mason. No record of other payments has ever been found.

Transfer of the collection to the Colorado Historical Society was arranged by Helen Chain of Denver, a well-known artist and close friend of William Henry Jackson. The catalogue for the collection was printed by the *Durango Herald*. Aside from the detailed list of the artifacts being acquired by the historical society, the catalogue bore Helen Chain's signature, reflecting her role in acquisition of the collection. Items were marked off as they were unpacked at the historical society.

Richard – and likely his father B.K. – sensed a new urgency to protect the resources after witnessing Charles McLoyd's activities during the Cliff Palace excavations. They also learned the value of institutional sponsorship and funding to support their activities as well as the difficulty of selling an entire collection. Members of the Wetherill family, labeled in later years as looters, were accused of burning roof beams during excavations, then at Cliff Palace of bursting holes in prehistoric walls to gain access to room blocks, or setting off dynamite with Gustaf Nordenskiöld to scare rattlesnakes. Some accusers went as far as to say they utilized dynamite to break through the walls to inner rooms.

In recently discovered letters to Julia Childs (an activist for the Indian Rights Association), Richard wrote on December 22, 1889, about his observations on that first visit to Cliff Palace.

From left: C.H. Green, Charles McLoyd, D.W. Ayers and Bob Allen reading 1889 *Durango Herald Mesa Verde Publication* 1891.

But to go on as I stated, in regard to the Cliff dwellers We have just commenced exploring, and studying the many ruins in the Mancos Canon, and but it is possible to throw any light upon this subject by diligent study, and labor, we intend to do it. I will give the coming year to this work, and I think by noting facts as we find them we can certainly derive some practical knowledge that will be of historical value. Already we have been very successful in finding relics.

Richard explained in detail burials, artifacts and ethnobotanical specimens found during excavations, then made a most significant observation.

…and they [the artifacts] were buried or hidden in such a manner as to indicate that the inhabitants put them away in haste, expecting to return. Our reason[s] for thinking this are these. In each end of the building are great holes broken in through the stone walls, evidently by besiegers for the purpose of driving out the inmates with greater facility, as the doors to these buildings are very small, averaging about 14 x 16 inches in size, of course some are smaller, and some a little larger but the majority of them are just large enough to allow a man to crawl in edge wise.

CHARLES McLOYD
AND HIS RESUME

On November 18, 1896, Charles McLoyd wrote to Charles R. Dudley of the Colorado State History Museum, offering a resume of his qualifications for curator for the collection he had been responsible for excavating in Mesa Verde.

> Denver Colo. Nov. 18th 96.
> Chas. R. Dudley
> Denver Colo.
>
> Dear Sir:
>
> I am anxious to secure the position of curator of the collections of the State Historical Society, and take the liberty of addressing you in regard to the matter. You will remember me when I inform you that I am the person who made the first collection of cliff-dwellers relics which attracted any attention, and which your society purchased from me, and which now forms a large part of the collection now in your room. I continued my investigations in the ruins of the Canon Country for some five or six years, making several other good collections, and think I can, without egotism, say I have as extended a practical knowledge of the ruins and relics as anyone. This would enable me to give an intelligent account of them to such visitors as might examine more collections. I will revive interest in the matter, and to in time add many valuable articles. You will understand the advantage of having the person who made the collection explain them to the public. And that my knowledge of the mines and the country in which they are found will enable me to interest your visitors. I can furnish the best of references in regard to honesty, temperance, and ability. Trusting this may receive your favorable attention, I am yours very respectfully.
>
> Chas. McLoyd
> 2028 California St. City

Note on envelope: "Return to Chas. McLoyd, 2028 California st., City Private"

Richard Wetherill noted in a letter dated two years later on January 2, 1891, his appreciation for Julia Childs' continued support.

> I have just received your welcome letter and your kind regard and well wishes expressed in the books sent us...
>
> It is of great encouragement for us to receive the well wishes of our Friends [*sic*] and to know that our work is not entirely un appreciated [*sic*] And from what you know of the Country, you can understand we are working against heavy odds. The pamphlets so kindly sent us by Dr. Childs have been of inestimateable [*sic*] value to us in giving us the proper method in which to carry on our work and give it Scientific value. Our last Winters Collection is now in Denver on exhibition in care of my Father and Brother – 1732 Champa Street. We supposed we could dispose of it there. Not because we want to. But more to give us means to carry on our explorations.

Aware of McLoyd's success in the sale of Cliff Palace artifacts, Richard and his brothers recognized the potential benefits of gathering and sell- ing a large collection. It would not only finance their excavations, but also hold to their Quaker beliefs through the study and preservation of cliff dwellings and their contents. In addition it could help sustain the family ranch. They understood that time was limited for retrieving objects after the purchase and publicity surrounding McLoyd's collec- tion. His success spurred numerous individuals to explore the Mesa Verde for profit – people who kept no journals and had little interest in preservation but a lot of interest in selling artifacts. Al referred to McLoyd's excavation technique as the "dusting out of the ruins." The McLoyd/Wetherill excavation partnership dissolved quickly after excava- tion of Cliff Palace even though professional communication continued. Each continued excavating, choosing his own methods, or lack thereof, and his own territory.

McLoyd turned toward rumored but yet unknown cliff dwellings tucked away in darkened alcoves of southeastern Utah's Grand Gulch. Richard Wetherill and his brothers explored deeper into the canyons of the Mesa Verde.

When B.K. Wetherill sought advice from the national museum, he included a handwritten copy of a journal kept by Richard with an exacting account of one day's excavation in Sandal House. The journal entry clearly demonstrates Richard's concern for contextual details as well as treatment of artifacts.

> The grave was filled with the same kind of debris as the pile outside; it was carefully cleaned out with shovels until some feath-

Richard packing a mule. This photo was taken by Frederick Chapin in 1889.

er cloth was struck then the hands were used to be sure that nothing should be broken or destroyed...

Current whereabouts of this journal are unknown, but when and if it is
found, it will not only dispel any notion of Richard as an ignorant cowboy
but also demonstrate that the family used proper excavation techniques
before the arrival of the Swedish scientist Gustaf Nordenskiöld.

Archaeological discoveries in Southwest Colorado not only changed the
agrarian focus of the Alamo Ranch, but also quickly penetrated the imagination of the American public. Tourists, guests, and scholars – most often
highly literate and educated – recognized the credibility and honesty of the
Wetherill family. Durango businessmen were first to arrive. Lawyer Ben
Ritter, who in 1891 would help arrange a permit for Gustaf Nordenskiöld
to enter and photograph the Ute reserve, was first to sign the Alamo Ranch
guest register. A parade of notable and historic figures followed from 1889
to 1902.

New train access to Mancos allowed the American public a chance to
view firsthand the 800-year-old stone ruins. A healthy national economy
made travel more feasible at the same time that Americans were taking
great interest in visiting, studying, excavating, and philosophizing on sub-

Frederick Chapin photo of Richard Wetherill, protecting the gear, preparing to dig.

Richard in Sandal House, 1889. Frederick Chapin photograph.

Richard Wetherill in west end of Sandal House, 1889. Frederick Chapin photograph.

BLM Anasazi Heritage Center

Gustaf Nordenskiöld

jects of anthropology and archaeology in the rapidly diminishing American wilderness. Relatively easy access to an area where they could view cliff dwellings and evidence of a "vanished race" existed nowhere else in the United States in the late 19th century. The Wetherill family and the Alamo Ranch benefited from the combination: access and interest.

The period between 1889 and 1897 – eight calendar years – was the heyday of the Alamo Ranch. Life was consumed with farming, ranching, politics, social activity, guided trips, and excavations. The involvement of John, Clayton, and, to a very limited extent, Win Wetherill, grew with increasing summer tourism demands.

Visitor numbers increased steadily through the summer months at the Alamo beginning in 1889. Mountaineer Frederick Chapin of Hartford, Connecticut, arrived on September 24, 1889. He made two visits to photograph dwellings, accompanied by C.P. Howard. Richard and Al did the guiding while the duties of packing fell upon their brother John. Chapin's glass plate photographs were the earliest, most complete, and detailed portraits of ruins within the Mesa Verde. He avoided using purple prose and romanticism so common to late 19th century writing. Chapin's perspective was through the eyes of a scientist. Trained in chemistry, he listened carefully to Richard Wetherill's stories and thoughts. Richard, in turn, shared with Chapin many of the "a-ha" moments in which he realized the meaning of his discoveries among the cliff dwellings. Chapin's publication in 1892 of *Land of the Cliff Dwellers,* was a hit then and the book remains in print over 100 years later.

Richard and his brothers collaborated on excavations during the winter of 1889-90. Between 1889 and 1893, they amassed or were involved with four different collections of Ancestral Puebloan artifacts. In every instance someone either hired them to dig artifacts or they followed the advice of Smithsonian Secretary Langley and gathered artifacts to sell as a collection themselves.

Among the Wetherills' distinguished visitors was Gustaf Nordenskiöld, who was referred to the family by premier botanist Alice Eastwood, of Denver. Eastwood had first visited the cliff dwellings on July 14, 1889, inscribing her name on a doorsill in Sandal House. A chance encounter

Inscription from Gustaf's parents to the Wetherills.

with Eastwood in the Denver library inspired the intellectually curious Nordenskiöld to travel farther west, meet the Wetherill family, and view the prehistoric cities in the cliffs. Richard first guided the Swedish scientist to excavation locations. He and his brother Al excavated initially for Nordenskiöld while John served as the appointed scribe for the excavation.

Collaborative expedition and excavation efforts were a given for the Wetherill brothers. Signatures placed by the brothers in alcoves or on ruin walls often consist of only the name "Wetherill." One brother would not usurp credit from the other. Much like the fictional Musketeers, they were all for one and one for all.

During his stay at the Alamo Ranch in 1891, Nordenskiöld purchased a new Kodak Brownie camera in Durango. Utilizing nitrate film in the Brownie, Al photographed alongside Nordenskiöld, at one point capturing the Swedish scientist's image as he prepared for a photograph under the black cover of his glass plate camera. Nordenskiöld later suggested a mutually beneficial trade with Al: in exchange for 100 individual pieces of pottery each with a distinct prehistoric design, Nordenskiöld would give him a complete album from the nitrate photographs. The young Swede quickly recognized the abilities of his Colorado hosts and a mutual respect and friendship developed between the Wetherills and the distinguished Nordenskiöld family. Gustaf's father sent the Wetherill family a large, hardbound book explaining their family history after his son's excavations with them.

After initial excavations in Mesa Verde, Nordenskiöld took his collection of artifacts to Durango to ship them, fully intending an uninterrupted journey home for them. He was arrested on orders initiated by Ute Tribal Indian Agent Charles Bartholomew. The arrest came as a complete shock. Charges related to Nordenskiöld's intended removal of antiquities from America and supposed illegal excavation of those artifacts within the Ute reservation. Richard and his family were appalled by their guest's arrest. Apparently, the American public could tolerate countless artifacts leaving canyons of the Mancos as long as they were taken by Americans. Having someone from a

WETHERILLS AND PHOTOGRAPHY

Richard learned from Chapin the art of glass plate (or wet-plate) photography. His curiosity led him to experiment with film developing as well as photographing the dwellings of the Mesa Verde and events around the Alamo Ranch. Before 1893, the Wetherills most likely relied on those who could afford the equipment to photograph the family. When Gustaf Nordenskiöld bought a second camera, for example, the brothers were able to take photos alongside their guest.

Fred Blackburn Collection/Courtesy of Charles Lang Jr.

Charles B. Lang, ca. 1890

Charles Lang, who was boarding with fellow photographer Charles Goodman in Bluff City, Utah, arrived at the Alamo Ranch in 1893. Lang was likely in the Bluff area as early as 1888 and had also gathered at least four of his own archaeological collections. He quickly established a friendship with B.K. and most likely made a trip to Cliff Palace, where he signed his name and the date, 1893, on a black cliff wall. Lang escorted Richard and his brothers to Cottonwood Wash in the winter of 1893.

Historian McNitt believed that Lang shot the photographs for the Wetherill 1893-1894 Hyde Exploring Expedition. But the Wetherills likely had acquired a Universal camera before that expedition and Richard was the photographer. He is absent in nearly all photographs of people from that trip. Richard was so enamored with photography that for a brief time he expanded his business by selling photographs in partnership with Lang between August 8, 1893, and November 9, 1894. He was quickly disillusioned when the costs became overwhelming, though, recording business expenses of $235.93. High costs and marginal income led to the demise of the business, but the family had gained valuable understanding of photography.

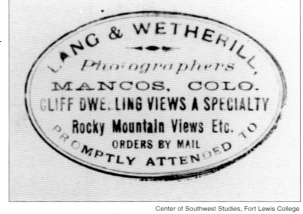

Lang and Wetherill photography stamp 1893

Center of Southwest Studies, Fort Lewis College

Balcony House photographed by Gustaf Nordenskiöld in 1891.
Note the glass plate carriers in the foreground.

foreign country remove such artifacts was, however, unconscionable. Nordenskiöld summarized his situation in a now infamous, terse telegraph to his father in Sweden, "Much trouble some expense no danger."

The episode helped provide the impetus for the Antiquities Act of 1906, aimed at protecting American artifacts. How much protection it would offer remained to be tested. Between 1906 and 1979 only one case utilizing the 1906 Antiquities Act would be successfully prosecuted in the state of Colorado. Since 1979, the law was superseded by another with a better record of prosecution, specifically the Archaeological Resources Protection Act or ARPA.

Nordenskiöld, after his arrest and release, returned to Mesa Verde to finish his excavations and photography. Then he wished to travel farther west into the land of the modern Pueblo people at Hopi. Richard and Al agreed to help, enlisting the services of a Navajo guide to ensure safe passage through hostile portions of the Navajo Reservation. Richard and Al's later penetrations deep into the Navajo and Hopi reservations allowed

A Nordenskiöld photograph of Richard Wetherill and John Wetherill looking in a crater.

Richard and his brothers to draw comparisons between modern Puebloan culture and the prehistoric culture represented in the cliff dwellings and other ruins. Richard never doubted that modern Pueblos were descendants of the Cliff Dwellers. He often drew comparisons between the two, based on his excavations and his observations at Hopi.

After Al's return from the Hopi Mesas, Richard saw a new opportunity for income and began his career as a trader. By 1894 he initiated trade in items of the Moqui – a slang term the Wetherill brothers used to refer to the Pueblo people of their day. It was derived from the Ute word *Moquitch*, which may have referred to both modern Pueblos and Ancestral Puebloans. Richard and his brothers' contacts expanded to the selling of pottery and baskets created by the people residing in the Hopi villages of Arizona.

Following his return to Sweden, the Wetherill family continued to write to Nordenskiöld about their most recent discoveries. In response, Nordenskiöld requested artifacts and ancient human skulls for his continued study.

Soon after Nordenskiöld's departure, Montezuma County Sheriff Adam Lewey arrested the Wetherill brothers as they were excavating in Mancos Canyon, and charged them with the same offenses as had been brought against Nordenskiöld. Articles in the Cortez *Montezuma Journal* referred to Nordenskiöld as "Count Grabenoff" while Richard was dubbed "Count Wetherill," a clear reference to their Swedish client. As had happened with the Swedish scientist, the case against the Wetherills was dismissed when witnesses failed to show for trial. Richard wrote Nordenskiöld in February of 1892 explaining the outcome.

> Amigo Mio
>
> As we have been having an experience similar to yours when [you were] here I thought best to await the outcome before writing you.
>
> As in your case – no witnesses appeared when our trial came off and so we are at liberty to continue as before till the "Locoed Agent" sees fit to make a fuss again. We have applied to the proper authorities for permission to do this kind of work regardless of the local croaking element.

Richard was soured by these events, and soon realized they were only the beginning of a long conflict with federal officials and local opinion. Federal harassment of the Wetherills was often driven by self-serving political interests pressing for change in the rampant excavation of southwestern artifacts. It wasn't that Richard would disagree with their concerns, but he was an inappropriate scapegoat for the accusations. Others who did collect artifacts without compunction continued while Richard was reviled. From the time he collaborated with Nordenskiöld, he became the target of

MR. LEWEY AND ARTIFACTS

Most interestingly, the offi-
cer who arrested the Wetherill
brothers, Sheriff Adam Lewey,
later served as a purchasing
agent for W.S. Crosby of
Colorado Springs in 1906,
and even in 1907 after there
was a law protecting antiquities. He was recruited by the
Colorado Cliff Dwellings
Association to purchase historic and prehistoric artifacts
within Montezuma County
for the Manitou Springs Cliff

Center of Southwest Studies/Fort Lewis College

Fake "cliff dwellings" at Manitou Springs.

Dwellings. Lewey was in charge of excavating the Blanchard Ruin, which resulted
in the removal of 44 boxcar loads of stone utilized to build the "cliff dwellings" at
Manitou Springs. In addition, he purchased several thousand dollars' worth of artifacts from individual collectors, including Mancos guide C.B. Kelly. The
Montezuma Journal described his effort.

> Adam Lewey made a trip to Bluff City a few days ago, to purchase
> Navajo blankets for the Cliff Dwellers [*sic*] Association at Colorado
> Springs. We did not learn how many he secured. This Association has
> gotten many Aztec and Indian relics from the country for their repro-
> duced Cliff house at Manitou. These curio [*sic*] will incracase [*sic*] in
> value as years go by, and will always bear the records of an ancient his-
> tory as they are now doing, and are rapidly becoming few in number.

Only a fraction of those artifacts ended up at Manitou Springs. The current
whereabouts of the rest are unknown.

defamation and harassment by government agents and scientists.

The H. Jay Smith Exploring Expedition financed by C.D. Hazzard provided Richard and his family a chance for national recognition both in
Minneapolis and later at Chicago's World's Columbian Exposition (a
world's fair dedicated to the 400th anniversary of Christopher Columbus'
1492 discovery of America, but held in the 401st anniversary year). At the
Chicago exposition, anthropological exhibits would be guided through the
vision of Frederick Ward Putnam, a proponent of public involvement in
archaeology.

H. Jay Smith of Milwaukee, art director for the Minneapolis Industrial

Battle Rock exhibit at the World's Columbian Exposition.

Exposition, and esteemed painter Alexis J. Fournier of Minneapolis, arrived at the Alamo Ranch on March 5, 1892. They returned again on December 5, 1892, with their benefactor C.D. Hazzard and Alice Palmer Henderson, both of Minneapolis.

Likely during the March visit John Wetherill led the Smith expedition through the canyons of the Mancos and southeastern Utah, finishing with a return trip up McElmo Canyon, which runs west from Cortez. Within the canyon are two prominent geologic features: Battle Rock (now known as Castle Rock and a part of the Canyons of the Ancients National Monument), and a large prominent rock island to the west and south which H. Jay Smith would name Battle Rock Mountain. Smith was captivated by the legends of gold buried below the mountain as well as by tales of battle and death occurring in prehistoric and historic times at both locations.

THE WORLD'S FAIR

The Chicago World's Fair would be grander than the exposition at Paris in 1889. The event would celebrate the discovery of America by Christopher Columbus in 1492, but would be delayed a year due to the enormity of required construction. Under the guidance and direction of architect Daniel H. Burnham, the White City would rise from a swampy wooded island landscape presenting to the world the beginnings of the Industrial Revolution in America. The city would be painted white in contrast to the dirty, blackened landscape of Chicago.

In Columbus' honor the event would be named the World's Columbian Exposition. Responding to the architectural wonder known as the Eiffel Tower from the Paris exposition in 1889, engineers would

Fred Blackburn Collection

The Ferris Wheel was a great engineering feat showcased at the Columbian Exposition.

choose the Ferris Wheel as their display of American engineering. Designed by W.G. George Ferris, the Ferris Wheel could carry up to 2,000 passengers at a time. Each state would have a building to exhibit its uniqueness in contributing to the American Dream.

Train fare rates, under pressure by fair management were lowered, allowing nearly 100,000 visitors a day to view the wonders inside. One special day held for the residents of Chicago saw nearly a million visitors. The Midway Plaisance exhibits were initially placed under the direction of Frederick Ward Putnam to house the anthropological and cultural exhibits.

Several events were not allowed in the White City. Buffalo Bill's Wild West Show and the Battle Rock exhibits by H. Jay Smith were held outside the entry gates of the White City. The fair had a lifespan of only six months, after which arsonists destroyed most of the major buildings.

Source: *The Devil in the White City*, by Erik Larson, published in 2003.

A stereoscope card of the St. Louis World's Fair exhibit.

In preparation for the exposition, Smith collaborated with Fournier – an artist in oils, watercolors, and pen and ink – as well as a photographer, a taxidermist, hunters, and guides. Fournier was one of the last of a group of Barbizon painters, realists who specialized in creating exacting scenes. They were replaced in the late 19th century when improvements in equipment enabled photographers to produce large, clearly defined images on glass. Fournier's job for Smith was to create background paintings for dioramas representing the archaeological sites.

With the Wetherills serving as guides and furnishing a large collection of antiquities, the end result would be an exhibit and catalogue for the Minneapolis exposition, largely of the Mancos ranchers' excavations. Smith would later expand this exhibit for the much larger World's Columbian Exposition in Chicago a year later.

Returning to Chicago, Smith initiated plans to build a replica of Battle Rock Mountain. Papier-mâché would not be enough. By rail from Montezuma County, he hauled plants, dirt, rock, and even a stuffed burro to be placed along a trail in the recreated scene from the Colorado canyon. Visitors were greeted by a variety of "caves" where artifacts and mummies were showcased in front of enormous dioramas painted by Fournier. They could follow the trail to the top of the mountain, or finish their "expedition" by exiting through a replicated kiva.

Richard went to Chicago to interpret his involvement in the exhibit for fair visitors. Among the many people he met there, he encountered a family he'd had dealings with in Colorado. Richard could hardly know when he

BATTLE ROCK MOUNTAIN

In *The Youths Companion*, September 1893, C.A. Stephens described the Battle Rock Mountain exhibit. Although rude in some instances by today's standards, his comments were quite acceptable to readers in 1892.

IN THE CLIFF DWELLERS' CAVE

Near the totem Poles of the Quakuhl Indians and the reproductions of ruins in Yucatan the World's Fair visitor encounters a mysterious and formidable structure, fifty or sixty feet high, and no less than two hundred feet long. It resembles a huge, reddish-brown rock, ledge, or butte, and is beetling and naked save for a few stunted pines and tufts of dry grass. This strange structure represents "Battle Rock," in southwestern Colorado. It is really an irregular frame of timber, covered over with sheet metal, dinted, bruised and painted to resemble rusty brown rocks.

Within it is ... a great dim, cool cave, walled by sandstone crags, – within which is exhibited a collection of a great number of articles connected with ... the prehistoric Cliff Dwellers – that vanished people who once built their stone villages far up on rocky shelves, beneath jutting cliffs, in the canons of Colorado, Utah and Arizona.

In the walls of the cavern the strange hamlets of this race are ingeniously reproduced in facsimile. They are made of stone and mortar, and are, as near as may be, the counterparts of the cave-dwellings which the explorers found in the now desolate deserts of the Southwest.

In another part of the cave are displayed the articles which have been found in the cliff-houses. They consist of more than two thousand samples of pottery, from large, coarse jars to cups and jugs which might well be coveted by bric-a-brac collectors; hundreds of stone hatchets, knives, arrowheads, hammers and mortars; bows, paddles, hoes, lances and plows of wood, and mantles woven from yucca fibre, wild cotton and the inmeshed feathers of turkeys ...

Here we can – if we like – view the bones of some of these extinct people – men, women and children who may have lived and died several thousand years ago. The high, dry recesses of the closed cliff-houses have preserved not only the bones, but the burial clothes in which the people were wrapped and laid to rest in carefully walled up niches of the crags.

The skulls give evidence that the Cliff Dwellers possessed average brain capacity. The skeletons show that the men were sometimes six feet in height, and the women five feet seven inches. The soft reddish brown hair of one of the women, which still adheres to a skull, is neither wiry like that of the Indian, nor kinky and black like that of the negro, but fine and straight. The remains, indeed, indicate that these denizens of pre-Columbian America may have been comely women and strong intelligent men.

saw the Hyde family in Chicago that their meeting would set in motion a series of events that would ultimately end his excavation career within Mesa Verde. Involvement with the Hyde family allowed Richard to expand his interests in exploration and understanding southwestern prehistoric people. Those investigations led him elsewhere in the Southwest.

After the 1893 exposition, the Wetherill brothers continued to guide on the Mesa Verde, but it was ultimately clear that Richard's interest did not lie with guiding greenhorns to Cliff Palace. Too many questions about lives of Puebloan people begged for answers in the back of his mind. Wanderlust quickly set in and willing museum donors eagerly offered financing to satisfy it.

Years earlier, Fred Hyde Sr., his sons Benny Talbot Babbit Hyde, and Fred Hyde Jr. had arrived from New York City shortly after Cliff Palace's discovery. Their subsequent tour of the cliff dwellings, followed by that second encounter at the World's Columbian Exposition in Chicago, led to Richard's lifelong entanglement with the heirs of the Babbo soap fortune, their eccentric habits and sporadic funding. Richard's Quaker diplomacy would be severely tested over the years he spent with the Hyde Exploring Expedition. Fred Hyde Jr. at one point presented Richard's widow Marietta with a large diamond in the hopes of wooing her toward marriage. The offer failed but the diamond heirloom is still held by the Wetherill family.

Richard's lack of interest in repeatedly guiding others is best demonstrated by how quickly his brothers Al, John, and Clayton inherited the job, while Richard moved to the periphery. Richard pioneered routes across the Navajo Reservation through Monument Valley into the canyons of the Tsegi where he discovered Keet Seel (now Navajo National Monument) in the company of his brothers. Soon they were following his lead while extending those routes across the West. Richard was allowed time to manage the ranch while freely expanding his knowledge and theories through focusing on his own excavations.

Richard received funding from the Hyde family to examine and reevaluate Charles McLoyd's excavations in southeastern Utah. Brothers Al and John had accompanied McLoyd to Grand Gulch during the winter of 1892. John had noted a difference in prehistoric skull types found within McLoyd's collection, unknowingly recognizing the Basketmaker as a "different race of people." Richard organized a Utah expedition and excava-

ANOTHER WORLD'S FAIR

Richard would attend one more World's Fair, held in St. Louis in 1904. While there he sold up to 300 Basketmaker objects – very likely the remainder of his family's Basketmaker artifacts – to Edward Seler, a curator from Berlin, Germany, where the collection now resides. Seler was an anthropologist who had worked in MesoAmerica.

tions based upon information provided by John and Al. What he found there led him to encourage Talbot Hyde's naming of the "Basket Makers" based on remains uncovered in Cave 7, Cottonwood Wash, during the winter of 1893-94. Richard published at least one article and likely two in *The Archaeologist* after 1893 Basketmaker excavations. One signed with "H" – likely for Hyde – discussed a flattened, highly polished stone with a jutting toe-like protrusion termed a "Sandal Last." The second article, signed by Richard, provided a review of their discoveries at Snider's Well located southwest of Cortez. Richard heard of Snider's Well on his return from the Basketmaker discoveries. A man, presumably Snider, thought the big depressions found there were water cisterns left by the Aztecs. He started to excavate only to find numerous random human remains scattered in the deep kiva depression. Richard's observations at this location are an example of his careful analysis of a site which is still worthy of further scientific study.

> At a depth of ten feet we came upon a mass of skeletons that had originally been thrown into the room in a haphazard manner. All of the skulls saved had each a hole in it such as would be made by striking it with a stone axe. Of twenty-five specimens examined, all proved to be of the cliff dwellers' type, having the perpendicular flattening at the back of the head.
> The skulls from the regular burial mounds in the vicinity have the oblique flattening upon the back of the head, showing there must be some distinction in the races.
> We infer from this discovery that these skeletons must have been prisoners or captives killed and thrown in this estufa.

Richard's excavation of this peculiar site was funded in part by C.C. Baldwin of Cleveland, Ohio, and fellow Quaker Robert K. McNeeley from Philadelphia, Pennsylvania. Both men purchased items from Richard.

Beyond Richard Wetherill's writings about what he uncovered at Snider's Well, another detailed description survives in Leander Hayes' journal. Hayes met Professor William Snider at a gathering in Mancos a few months after Snider's discovery of the burial while digging for water on his property, and subsequently visited the site in April 1894.

Hayes was very familiar with the work of the Wetherills when he visited the site during their excavation yet he identified them only as two "experts." From his Snider's Well excavations Richard Wetherill identified a third "type" of Ancestral Puebloan people, characterizing the resident culture found here as Valley Dwellers. He based his theory on a distinct angle of cradle board deformation among these people which differed significantly from the Cliff Dwellers' cradle board deformation and from Basketmakers' normal skull shapes.

Hayes' journal provides a detailed description of the kiva and burial.

Mr. Snider said that there were no indications on the surface of a ruin beneath. It was convenient to his house. So he simply risked finding water there. When they found the mass of Human bones, they stoped work, and did no more that fall, nor winter, nor until the next spring. Two weeks before our visit, haveing secured the assistance of two experts, they had opened it. Or at least part of it to the light of day.

... Imagine a well twenty feet in diamiter, a great round hole in the earth twenty feet across it & eighteen feet deep. This was our first view of it. All this dirt had been removed, a long shaky slender lader was our only means of getting down into it.

The room is seemingly a perfect circle eighteen feet in diamiter. ... The floor seemed to be a cement. The wall is only about four feet high a very heavy wall built of flat stones. The wall is about twenty inches thick, and of good workmanship. Eight piers, or Butrasess are built to the wall at intervals around the room. These indicate the design of sustaining great weight. The wall and piers are in a perfect state of preservation.

It appears that heavy timbers had rested on the wall, comeing together at the top, and all leaning to the centre, in the shape of a cone, portions of these timbers yet remain, but so decayed they would not bear handling. I wondered, who did all this, when, why under ground. What became of them. The wall is covered, not with plaster, as the round room in the Cliff Palace [referring to Kiva D], but with a peculier coating, of which I secured a few small pieces. This coating is about one eighth of inch thick, and with a good glass I can count 9 to 11 coats, apparently, differing in colors. I got these home safely.

At intervals, around the wall and built so in laying the rock are little openings like small ovens, or closets, without doors. All the same size and shape, and the same distance from the floor, all skilfuly made. They are about twelve inches in heigth, by ten inches in width, and extend about twelve inches back into the wall. Each one about twelve inches from the floor. All neatly coated like the wall.

These are identical with those I saw in the beautiful plastered round room in Cliff Palace, save the coating. This impresses me as the two being of one race of people. However so great a difference there be in their homes. There was a great pile of human bones on the floor and piled up against the wall. Against the wall they were about two feet deep [Photographs of this skeletal material are a part of the American Museum of Natural History collection from the Hyde Exploring Expedition of 1894], then they extended out from the wall about four feet, and in length about six feet. Lying all around on the top of the wall were whole human skulls, and many of the large bones of those Ancient people. There was allso a large pile lying on the surface outside.

Quite a quantity of broken potery was lying around in this room. Painted potery, allso corrugated potery, these are identical with all I found in all other ruins.

In removeing the debris, the accumulation of doubtless of many centuries, the workmen noticed that the main wall sudenly stoped. There was a break off, then about two feet further on the wall began again. Upon exhamination, this proved to be a narrow hall way, perhaps connecting this with another room, or rooms, yet to be found. This hall is about two feet wide, by four feet high, tis very neatly walled with flat stones, and covered over the top with small poles. Question. What has preserved them, when the larger ones decayed. This hall way had been opened about six feet back from the room. The wall extending on yet further.

Mr. Snider requested me to go into it and with his trowel see how very tight the dirt is packed. I did so, and found it very difficult to make an impression on it, it was so dry and packed. I secured a fine, but small collection of relics here. I wanted one of the Skulls, but Mr. Snider would not part with it. Not even one. [Richard Wetherill reported saving these skulls] However he made up a collection for me of their bones from the pile on the outside Allso some fine specimens of potery Some quite large pieces.

Richard sporadically guided to the Mesa Verde after 1894 but his focus turned to southeastern Utah, Arizona, New Mexico, and Mexico. A trip in 1896 led him to his final home at Pueblo Bonito, Chaco Canyon, New Mexico (where his life would tragically end in 1910). While on this extended trip Richard stopped at Montezuma Castle near Camp Verde, Arizona, on March 6, 1896. While there he excavated an area he recognized as having been missed by prior exploration:

To-day I visited the old Cliff dwelling, known as the old fort, and is the one so graphically described by Charles Lumis.

Richard described the ruin in detail, going on to explain his discovery.

At the east end of this tier of rooms is a small ledge 25 feet long and 1 or 3 feet wide. It adjoins the row of rooms, and over it all have to pass to ascend to the rooms above. In this small space I found, after a few minutes' work, the remains of at least a half dozen children, one of which is a very fair mummy. All of these were in a promiscuous mass and nothing with them. The mummy was the lower burial, and it rested in a very small excavation next to the rock on the floor of the cave. It was laid straight out: head to the east: face up: hand at its sides. A bowl was found at the left of the head, and a small bow and arrows were lying lengthwise at the right side. The body is wrapped in cotton cloth, which is still in a state of good preservation. The grave was covered with small, round sticks placed three or four inches apart, and parallel with each other, supporting a rush mat which had been spread over the grave. Over all this was about two feet of debris, among which was found so many other remains...

Richard Wetherill was 38 years of age in 1896. A steady supply of young women – possibly traveling with their families or especially unmarried school teachers of the proper Victorian era – flowed through the door of the Alamo Ranch. Among those guests were potential wives for Richard. Julia Cowing of New York, Marcia Billings of Denver, and finally Mamie Palmer of Burdette, Kansas, all captured his interest. Richard visited Cowing in New York after attending the World's Columbian Exposition in Chicago, but his side trip did not result in marriage. He asked Wirt Jenks Billings to accompany him as stenographer to Grand Gulch in 1893, possibly with the hope of attracting his sister, red-haired Marcia. Julia Cowing's brother Bert tagged along on the 1897 trip to Grand Gulch.

The arrival of a band-wagon at the Alamo Ranch would finally provide an opportunity for marriage. Sydney Laverne Palmer and his family held an interest in music, photography, and anthropology. Talented musicians, they paid for their cross-country travel by

BLM Anasazi Heritage Center

Marietta Palmer and her family ca. 1892.

From left: Richard Wetherill, B.K. Wetherill, unknown Ute, unknown, Bert Cowing, Mancos Jim, Teddy Whitmore, Mrs. Jim, George Bowles, unknown Ute, Orian Buck.

staging concerts in towns and cities along their route. Prior to their arrival at the Alamo Ranch in September of 1895 they staged a concert for the townspeople of Cortez.

Richard and his brother Win both took a shine to one of the Palmer girls, Marietta, known as Mamie. Marietta was much nearer Win's age than Richard's, triggering a conflict that the family resolved by sending Winslow to Quaker school at Oskaloosa, Iowa. The Palmer family was Quaker, and Richard sensed an acceptable arrangement. But their first encounter was not magic according to Marietta. Returning from a trip to the snake dance at the Hopi Village of First Mesa in northeastern Arizona disheveled and unshaven, Richard proved less than an attraction initially. He quickly turned to duties of guiding the family, parking their bandwagon on the wagon road through Mancos Canyon below Sandal House, where he wooed Mamie and the young woman inscribed her name on the wall. Richard likely took the family to Balcony House, Cliff Palace, and Spruce Tree House as well. Mamie's signature remains on the back wall of an upper story room within Balcony House.

Richard followed the family's bandwagon to San Francisco, where he and Mamie Palmer were married on December 8, 1896. They spent their honeymoon in southeastern Utah's Grand Gulch. The first woman known to have entered this remote canyon since Ancestral Puebloan times, Mamie held her own among the all-male excavation crew. Richard and Mamie moved from the Mancos Valley to Chaco Canyon in 1897, where Richard had begun excavations the year before with Dr. George Pepper, representing the American Museum of Natural History in New York City. Richard would die of bullet wounds in 1910. Events surrounding his death remain suspect, even though the Navajo man who was accused of shooting him, Chischilly Biye', served five years for it. (See epilogue for further information.)

Marietta Palmer Wetherill

The Honeymoon. From left: Orian Buck, James Etheridge sitting, George Hairgrove, Levi Carson, Marietta Wetherill, Teddy Whitmore, Charlie Mason bathing face, and either Hal Eaton or George Bowles standing in Cave 7, Grand Gulch, 1897.

BENJAMIN ALFRED (AL) WETHERILL

THE BALD-HEADED
SMART ALEC

B enjamin Alfred Wetherill, better known to all as Al, was born on June 25, 1861, in Leavenworth, Kansas. He would die 88 years later in Sand Springs, Oklahoma, a long way from where his heart lay. Richard and Al worked closely together in those early years. Richard was three years older but as eldest sons of B.K. and Marian, their duties were more rigidly defined than those of the younger children.

Al Wetherill as a young man in Atchison, Kansas.

Al later recounted the story of his family's move to Leavenworth on a steamboat route as no bridges or railroad yet existed there. He wrote that his father first operated a grocery store, then worked for the Osage Agency and finally in the boom days of lead mining in Joplin, Missouri. While in Kansas, Al worked for the Atchison, Topeka & Santa Fe Railroad. His letter of recommendation upon leaving their employ in 1881 at the age of 20 to move with the family to Mancos remains in the family collection. Their move west of the Missouri River to Mancos placed the family as Quaker pioneers in western Colorado. Al recorded how the children thoroughly enjoyed the trip, having to be reined in to keep them near their tent camps along the way. Many friendships Al had formed in Leavenworth and Atchison were maintained through correspondence in the years to follow.

"The Bald-Headed Smart Aleck" was a term of endearment for Al, coined by Irish editor W.H. "Muldoon" Kelly of the *Mancos Times*. Kelly, a tell-it-as-it-is type of editor, held a special place in his heart for the Alamo Ranch and the family who lived there. He especially enjoyed ribbing Al in his local news and gossip column.

Al Wetherill was much more outgoing and social than his brothers. He interacted well with the rest of the community, joining and attending various fraternal organizations. His sense of humor is apparent in his writing. Often separated from his wife Mary Tarrant and daughter Martha Cecelia, Al wrote numerous letters, starting them with "My Dear Darned Family" or "Dear Fambily." He would then go on to describe in detail encounters with people and his non-judgmental yet often humorous observations of those around him. He often signed his name "Pop" or "Pops," adding a figure of an imp or other small drawings. Inscription documentation work in the canyons revealed that Al often drew imps or other caricatures next

From left: Clyde Colville, Al Wetherill, and John Wetherill playing Chinese checkers at Kayenta, Arizona, ca. 1940. This was Al's last visit with John.

to his inscription "Wetherill" with no first name. Al's imps are a trademark of sorts when identifying the inscriber or the writer. Al wrote an understated note on the ledge below Inaccessible House in the present-day Ute Mountain Ute Tribal Park that read, "We got in there Ye need not try, Al." He also may have left a prophetic inscription in pencil on a Spruce Tree House beam. Inscription:

> "All ye should that wander here Be better men, your time is near go think it over"

Al was the last to leave the Alamo Ranch, continuing his guiding to the Mesa Verde until 1902. He also was the last brother to die, a hard duty for Al, who missed his brothers in his later years. His early years on the Mesa Verde followed with exploration of the Four Corners region were the cornerstone of his life.

Al's fate, like brother Richard's, upon reaching the Mancos land selected by B.K. was to create an infrastructure for the family. While building fences and irrigation canals they encountered remains from prehistoric Puebloan people, their predecessors in the Mancos Valley. Al's explanation of their connection with their predecessors is best recorded in his own words.

> Our first knowledge of the existence of the Cliff Dwellings was

not in the finding of the buildings but through a gradual step up from the abundance of ruins of other Prehistoric buildings which were scattered everywhere around the Mancos Valley and indicated by the mounds which were formed by the fallen walls of a race which existed at some unknown earlier date and were generally classed as Aztecs. For some reason never explained as then there was no similarity between the Aztec ruins in Old Mexico and these scattered villages and individual wrecked houses.

Al's visit to Sandal House likely preceded that of Richard in 1882. Al recorded riding to Sandal House on a pony named Dante after receiving word of a cliff dwelling about 12 miles down-canyon. He reminisced that he wished to be a storybook cowboy, choosing to ride to the site without grub or sleeping blanket. His adventure proved more than he bargained for, as he reached the cliff dwelling that was carefully hidden away 100 feet above the Indian trail. He had hoped to pick up some pottery sherds or arrowheads on his visit. Lateness of the hour required that he sleep wrapped in a saddle blanket on a flat rock. Romance found in such cowboy life was quickly dispelled as the warm sun setting in the west was replaced by bone-chilling cold creeping down the narrow valley. Canyon convection is a common occurrence in the Southwest. Much like air convection within a chimney, warm air slips upward to the mesa tops while cold air rushes to fill the void. Al's night was miserable. Chilled and hungry, he likely concentrated on returning home after he was revived by the first rays of morning sun.

Al indicated that shortly after visiting Sandal House the family was contacted by military officers from Fort Lewis who wanted to scout the little known canyon country of the Mancos River. The military post was located east and south of the Alamo Ranch along the La Plata River. Captain Baker, instigator of the expedition, was impressed by the brothers, the canyon, and the archaeology. Likely this date was 1883. Al recorded it as the first of many excursions by the military and the Wetherill family in exploration of the cliff dwellings. Al accompanied Richard and Surgeon Comfort of the Fort Lewis military station on a visit to dwellings within the canyon in late spring or early summer of 1885 – he wrote many years later that it happened in 1887, but inscription evidence contradicts that date. Al separated from his brother and Comfort to explore Cliff and Soda canyons, abandoning his horse and traveling by foot. It was a wise choice, as livestock entry to the high cliff dwellings was impossible.

Following an arduous route, Al was likely reminded of stories told by oxen freighters the prior year about ruins located deep in Soda or Cliff canyon. Al's information derived from two possible informants. George W. Jones, a well-known oxen freighter from Aztec, New Mexico, and Durango, Colorado, who often hauled freight for the mines around Silverton and

William Henry Hayes obtained one more bit of notoriety in 1892 when he formally complained to Ute Indian Agent Charles Bartholomew about Wetherill excavations along the Mancos River. Hayes' charge resulted in the brothers' arrest and subsequent court appearance. It was ironic, considering how many artifacts Hayes likely helped remove when accompanying Osborn in 1884.

Rico, is the most likely source. In the canyons of the Mesa Verde, Jones was accompanied by prospector and local judge William Henry Hayes of Mancos and S.E. Osborn of Burlington, Iowa. Hayes, a local prospector, assisted Osborn in a survey for coal deposits. A second individual familiar with the canyons was T.W. Wattles, a Mancos resident and relative of Eugenia and Hilda Faunce, sisters who later married Clayton and Winslow Wetherill. Other notes from Al record that men – very likely the Osborn group – told him of the removal of an intact weaving from a loom within a cliff dwelling in Soda Canyon. On his trip in 1885, Al named the unique and isolated cliff dwelling from whence the textile was removed "The Balcony House."

Traveling alone, Al found what Osborn had reported, what is now known as Hemenway House 2 located high on the canyon wall. Hemenway House 2 – or as Al knew it from his prior contacts, the Brownstone Front – is readily visible from the modern overlook at Balcony House. Al and his brothers returned to Hemenway House 2 in July to complete the family's first excavation of a cliff house, leaving names and dates etched on a stone slab within the ruin.

Al's footsteps from his solitary explorations can be retraced today by following his inscribed name in three locations: Hemenway Houses 1 and 2 and Balcony House. He recalled in his writings that he avoided visiting many smaller dwellings, choosing instead to seek large visible structures located a thousand feet above him under protected overhangs of the Cliff House sandstone. Al first visited Hemenway 1. While there, he could not have missed the numerous inscriptions left on masonry by earlier explorers and excavators. The cliff dwelling proved to be a prelude for the condition of ruins Al found: prior excavation and removal of artifacts by earlier individuals or groups. Numerous inscriptions on stone masonry demonstrate that S.E. Osborn and his men thoroughly searched the major cliff dwellings in 1884 before the Wetherills' first visit.

Farther up Soda Canyon Al viewed the Brownstone Front, (now known as Hemenway 2) a name Virginia Donaghue McClurg later misapplied to Balcony House. McClurg founded the Colorado Cliff Dwellings Association, a group of Colorado women who through years of hard work and political wrangling initiated legislation responsible for designating

TWO HEMENWAY HOUSES

There are two cliff dwellings called Hemenway House, resulting in some confusion.

The first, Hemenway 1, is located in the Ute Mountain Ute Tribal Park on the *west* side of Soda Canyon. This site is often confused with Nordenskiöld House, which is located slightly north of Hemenway 1 on the same level.

The second Hemenway is located north and up-canyon of Hemenway 1 on the *east* wall of Soda Canyon (across and down-canyon from Balcony House). This second Hemenway contains two cliff dwelling sections, Hemenway 2 and Little Hemenway, both of which were known by prospector S.E. Osborn and Al Wetherill as the Brownstone Front. The issue is further complicated by Cliff Dwellings Society founder Virginia McClurg, who referred to Balcony House as the "Brownstone Front."

Hemenway 1 was named at Jesse Fewkes' "Camp Science," held in September of 1901 within Soda Canyon to determine the fate of Mesa Verde cliff dwellings. Hemenway 2 was named in 1907 by Edgar L. Hewett, then field archaeologist for the Archeological Institute of America. Fewkes initially chose in 1901 to honor Mary Hemenway by naming the cliff dwelling on the west side of Soda Canyon after her. However, once the boundaries of the national park were drawn in 1906, that Hemenway House was outside the park on Ute Mountain Ute tribal lands. So Hewett chose another dwelling farther up the east side of the canyon – and thus within the park – to name in Hemenway's honor. Thus, there are two cliff dwellings with the same name, one in the national park and one in the Ute Mountain Ute Tribal Park.

Both were named in honor of Mary Hemenway for her financial support of the first organized archaeological research trip in the Southwest. The cliff dwellings' namesake never set foot in Mesa Verde. She did sponsor numerous

ethnographic expeditions to the modern Pueblos. Adolph Bandelier, among other early ethnologists, Hewett, and Fewkes were beneficiaries of the Hemenway Southwestern Expeditions.

Hemenway House 2 ca. 1890.

BLM Anasazi Heritage Center

Mrs. Ben Ritter, second from left, and friends on balcony at Balcony House.

Mesa Verde as a national park. Climbing to Brownstone Front/Hemenway 2, Al viewed Balcony House across the canyon, later characterizing it as the most noticeable ruin anywhere along the main canyon. He noted that Balcony House had been ransacked, contradicting Osborn, who had written that his party left all the artifacts as they had found them in 1884. In reality, though, Osborn was using freighter George W. Jones to remove artifacts from the dwellings, and coal from the geologic seams; where they ended up is unknown. Osborn's assertion, written in 1886, was more likely in response to a claim by McClurg, who wrote in the *Denver Post* that her feet, in 1886, were the first to touch centuries of dust on the prominent architectural balcony feature.

Intrigued by the beauty of Balcony House, Al completed his second 1,000-foot descent from the Brownstone Front/Hemenway House 2, crossed the canyon and climbed up to Balcony House. Finding more disturbance by earlier parties, Al continued at the same level below the cliff and up-canyon to a slot just north of Balcony House. A route he found there allowed access to the rim. Despite being tired, Al hurried through the waning daylight west across the mesa, dropping into the head of Cliff Canyon, where he worked his way over boulders, brush, and fallen logs down-canyon. Judging by the outlet he observed while passing along the main canyon route to the Brownstone Front/Hemenway House 2, he was sure this side canyon would eventually meet the main fork of Cliff or Soda canyons. Lateness of day accompanied by a rigorous three-ruin tour was followed by the tough climbs out of Soda Canyon and into Cliff Canyon. Al was approaching exhaustion when he turned and spied Cliff Palace – the first of his family to do so.

> I happened to look up the cliff on the West side of the Canon and over the treetops along the slope I saw the upper of the Cavern and the tops of some of the walls of what is now known as Cliff Palace.

Al most likely was on the west side of the canyon, looking east toward Cliff Palace. He never claimed to have entered Cliff Palace in 1885. He had already gone into three other cliff dwellings by the time he spotted it, and all of them had been ransacked. It would have been logical for him to assume Cliff Palace had been as well. Add to that the difficulty of getting to Cliff Palace, and Al apparently decided it wasn't worthwhile to go back that day.

When he reported his discoveries to Richard and Dr. Comfort at the end of that long day, Al noted a general disinterest on their part. Perhaps it was because he told them the other dwellings he'd entered had been ransacked. For whatever reason, no one placed much importance on the last cliff dwelling he sighted that day. All he eventually wished for was that the record would show his sighting of the structure three years before the oft-described "discovery" by Richard, Charlie, and perhaps Acowitz. Based on other inscriptions in nearby cliff dwellings, S.E. Osborn or his men likely entered Cliff Palace in 1884, making the question of which Wetherill saw it first a moot point. Yet for the rest of his life Al regretted not going back to explore Cliff Palace. His inability to summon up the energy required to get to and examine that massive site haunted him. Al reflected in later years on this "near miss" of a discovery.

> The actual value of being first can be beyond the power of the dollar mark and as a lasting value is well illustrated through all history. It is not of much satisfaction to go around and boast of what you have seen or of the results you have accomplished. It will all show up in the years to come.
>
> ... Such a simple thing it seems now to say I have done this or that but to prove it…satisfactorily…you may have a wonderful memory or notes and dates of what is mostly forgotten by the interested public.
>
> ... Such a small matter as the discovery of an ancient building, oddly constructed and deserted for more than 1400 years….What we want to know now is how and when the ruins of the building known as Cliff Palace was first actually discovered by white men.

Al was the family scribe. He wrote notes on envelopes, paper bags, and recycled bits of paper. He especially enjoyed writing poetry, producing volumes that were often in demand by his nieces and nephews. They remembered his recitations, writing him to request a certain piece from their childhood.

In 1889 the Wetherill family was exhibiting artifact collections in Pueblo and Denver. The public wasn't as interested as the family had hoped, at least not until Charlie Mason and Clayton Wetherill returned from excavations in Cliff and Soda canyons with the mummified remains of a child intact within a cradleboard. Although grisly, the mummy generated substantial interest, an emotional sight for viewers. Quaker language is evident in this poem, with Al's use of "thou" and "thy," likely chosen by Al with respect for the discovery, emphasizing his feelings when viewing the macabre exhibit.

> Greetings, child of an ancient race.
> How little is told by thy baby face
> Of children's joys and a mother's tears
> All lost now for a thousand years.
>
> Thy once bright eyes beheld great things.
> Thou's hope of parents that childhood brings.
> Yet thou, with others of thy race,
> Were doomed to pass; leave but a trace.
>
> None there are who can thy story tell.
> All are gone where thou didst dwell.
> All voices stilled; All lips are sealed,
> Forever closed and unrevealed

Another example found within Al's writing reveals the influence of his Quaker beliefs and religious upbringing on his explorations and discoveries.

> It was so much like treading "holy ground" to go into those peaceful-looking homes of a vanished people. It is something you have to experience to appreciate. It recurred again and again as we found new houses, untouched through all those long years. We knew that if we did not break into that charmed world someone else would, sometime – someone who might not love and respect those emblems of antiquity as we did. It was a strange feeling: perhaps all this had been given into our keeping until someone else might do it more capably than we.

Al broke into that world on a Hyde Exploring Expedition to the caves of southeastern Utah organized by Richard in 1893. They reached a site that had been explored by Warren K. Moorehead and the Illustrated American

Exploring Expedition the year before. Al noticed a discoloration in the soil containing charcoal and cultural material below the previously known layers. He dug and followed the discoloration to nearly four feet below the upper level of the Cliff Dwellers occupation. Al's initial discovery of one human burial was soon multiplied by 96 more. The exploring party uncovered a mass of burials along with their first discovery of earlier basketry. As John later wrote, the Hyde Exploring Expedition members of 1893 and 1894 changed the entire chronology of the Ancestral Puebloan by their analyses.

We knew when we had finished with this cave that by the articles buried with them and the shape of the skull that we had a different people from the Cliff Dwellers, but we did not know where to place them. We went from Hammond Canyon to Grand Gulch. After we had worked a few days we found a mummy in dry dust. And then we knew for certain that we had a tribe different than the Cliff Dwellers. They did not live under the cliffs but used them to bury under and to cache surplus supplies.

In 1893 identifying the Basketmakers changed direction for the Alamo Ranch, with the ranching duties becoming secondary in the Wetherills' 18-year (1884 to 1902) self-imposed responsibility for the ruins of the Mesa Verde. Richard, Clayton and John would carry their Inward Light-inspired sense of responsibility to the remnants of those ancient cultures well into the 20th century, long after their departure from the Mesa Verde to other areas of the Four Corners. Al addressed the Inward Light of his belief, reflecting on why archaeology played such an enormous role in the family's lives.

It all reverts back, of course, to the fact that no one told us to do it. Any hardships were our own responsibility, But, we could not shake off the feeling that we were possibly predestined to take over the job, knowing what depredation had been committed by transients who neither revered nor cared for the ruins as symbols of the past.

Al, as well as Richard, developed an interest in photography, taking many of the Wetherill family photographs within Mesa Verde and elsewhere, on glass plate or nitrate film. His family actually kept the wooden-cased glass plate "Universal" camera, made by the Rochester Optical Company, of Rochester, New York, and the tripod the Wetherills used for photography upon the Mesa Verde. It is now stored with the Wetherill Family Archives at the Anasazi Heritage Center, near Dolores, Colorado.

Over the years all the brothers would guide clients across the Four Corners. Al, Richard, John, and Clayton worked hard together gathering the 1889 and 1890 collections. Al was with Richard guiding Frederick

Photograph of Al Wetherill at Walpi, 1891, taken by Gustaf Nordenskiöld.

Al Wetherill's glass plate camera used in Mesa Verde.

Chapin and Howard in 1889. He and Richard conducted limited excavations with Nordenskiöld. Al guided Nordenskiöld across expanses of the Navajo reservation to the Colorado River in 1891, viewing for his first time the powerful Hopi Snake Dance and the vast dimensions of the Grand Canyon. His experience guiding T. Mitchell Prudden deep into present-day Escalante/Grand Staircase National Monument in Utah and a brief view of the Colorado River opened up a whole new world for the Wetherill family. Al wrote:

> The rest of the journey was through uninhabited tracts. The few people we encountered surveyed us with astonished looks. We were three ragged figures on wretched horses, riding along at a slow walking pace.

Al developed two special clients among the many who visited the Alamo Ranch. First and foremost was a deep and abiding friendship he formed with the grand dame of botany, Alice Eastwood, the woman who had sent Nordenskiöld to the Alamo Ranch in 1891. Many have wondered if there was more than friendship between Alice and Al on their wide-ranging excursions collecting plants. No one need worry about improprieties. Alice quite frankly explained their situation to a Mormon woman in Moab, Utah, after she and Al had completed a long and dry trip by horseback from the Thompson Springs railhead in Utah, located on the main route through Salt Lake between Denver and San Francisco.

Alice Eastwood ca. 1910.

Al, notified of Alice's anticipated arrival in Utah, left the Alamo Ranch trailing a remuda of horses and pack mules. It was not an easy trek from the Alamo Ranch, a distance of nearly 200 miles. A Quaker in Mormon country, Al arrived as Alice departed the ramp at the isolated whistle-stop outpost. Journeying south through the alkaline Cisco Desert, they hoped to find respite along the way. They arrived in Moab, and went in search of accommodations. Alice and Al were greeted by a correct and proper Mormon woman who inquired as to their marital status. Alice informed the woman that she was married to botany and had little time or desire for other pursuits. Together they collected more than 500 species of plants on a single trip and compiled the first botanical collection from southeastern Utah.

Alice later left Denver to accept an appointment to the California Academy of Science. Correspondence regarding Al and Alice's earlier years of exploration was destroyed in the 1906 San Francisco earthquake. Alice was able to retrieve her extensive rare botanical collection by going in and out of the crumbling, burning building. Replaceable plant species, along with her personal correspondence and belongings, went up in smoke. Hearing of the disaster, several of the Wetherill brothers visiting Charlie Mason in Washington state made a side trip with the hope of assisting Alice after the disaster. Through her tenacity, she rebuilt her voluminous plant collection for the California Academy of Science.

Al maintained a lifelong friendship with Eastwood, as did his daughter and wife after his death in 1950. Eastwood often sent special gifts to Al's

Mary Tarrant Wetherill and daughter Martha.

daughter Martha Cecelia, and her sons.

Alice had first visited Cliff Palace in July of 1889, earlier than her biography reports. When she arrived, excavations by the Wetherill brothers were in progress. Alice collected plants under a pinyon and juniper canopy, in a protected alcove, and by a seeping spring around and above Cliff Palace while the brothers worked in the immense structure. Al learned quickly the difference between rare and common plants. His treks included discovery of plant species heretofore unknown to Alice. Al pressed and sent new species to Alice in her absence. Impressed by never-before-seen botanical specimens and the Wetherills themselves, Alice named several species of these plants *wetherilli* in their honor.

The second prominent visitor was Dr. Theophil Mitchell Prudden, who arrived at the Alamo Ranch in 1895. He began a lifelong friendship with the Wetherill family and what would grow into nearly 10 years of exploring the Colorado Plateau. Prudden, a medical doctor who pioneered the scientific fields of histology and pathology, became fascinated with both prehistoric and historic cultures found in the Southwest.

Born in Middlebury, Connecticut, Prudden completed his education at Yale. T.M., as he signed his name and was called by the Wetherills, spent little time on Mesa Verde. He chose instead to use the Alamo Ranch as a base for exploration and excavation deep into southern Utah, northeastern Arizona and northwestern New Mexico, with some excavation work south of Cortez and Mitchell Springs. The report of his expeditionary work, *On the Great American Plateau,* was published in 1906.

In 1895, Al and Richard guided Prudden to the Hopi village of Walpi with the help of Jim Joe, the Bluff, Utah, Navajo who may have helped guide Nordenskiöld in 1891. Photographic attempts failed but the journey was recorded in detail by W.H. "Muldoon" Kelly who was ecstatic to accompany the expedition. Exploration with Prudden after 1895 was led by Al and/or Clayton.

Al returned to the Grand Canyon in 1897 with Prudden. Accompanied by his brother Clayton, and a succession of Navajo, Ute, and Paiute guides, Al followed a portion of a route he'd taken in 1891 with Nordenskiöld, that had been shown to them by a Mormon miner named Seth Tanner. Al, Clayton, and Prudden for the first time crossed the Colorado

BLM Anasazi Heritage Center

T. Mitchell Prudden

PRUDDEN'S PRAISE

In a letter published by Yale University Press in 1927, T.M. Prudden praised the Wetherill brothers.

Quite contrary to the practice of most of the "pot hunters," as they have been recently called, the excavations controlled by them [the Wetherills] were conducted with the utmost care and conservatism, careful records and descriptions being made.

The learned men of the day seemed to care nothing for the pots or the ruins, and no funds were forthcoming them from the Government or from other sources to make investigations.

The Wetherills, however, were early impressed with the scientific aspects of the matter, and while they have been often identified by ignorant critics with the earlier devastations, they were in fact most eager and persistent in preserving from harm the great ruins of the Mesa Verde, as well as others, through a series of years, in which they were neglected by the archaeologists, ignored by the Government authorities and sorely threatened by the tourists who often visit them with predatory intent.

Photograph of Al Wetherill and possibly Jim Joe, taken by Gustaf Nordenskiöld.

**Roe Ethridge, Al Wetherill and Seth Tanner on the Colorado River in 1891.
This photograph was taken by Gustaf Nordenskiöld.**

Al and miner Seth Tanner on the Colorado River. Gustaf Nordenskiöld photograph.

River at both Hite and Lee's Ferry crossings. They ended their trip as guests in the home of the Hopi leader Tom Pollaca. Their expeditions were the first commercial exploration of what would become Escalante/Grand Staircase National Monument almost a century later. Prudden, like Frederick Chapin, viewed the cultures they studied with a scientific eye, offering glimpses into the emerging southwestern science of archaeology and ethnology, once again through the quiet guidance and advice of the Wetherill family.

Numerous guests of similar stature came and went from the Alamo Ranch, but few made such long-term commitments to anthropological and archaeological study of the area as did Prudden. By 1896 Richard was in Chaco. John would remain in Mancos until 1900, but was farming on his own, or off on prospecting expeditions with his father-in-law John Wade. Ranch and guiding duties increasingly fell on the quickly balding head of the Smart Aleck, Al.

Despite several distinguished visitors, Mancos remained a lively frontier town, according to the journal of Leander Hayes, a Presbyterian minister who visited Mancos in 1893-94. Hayes, who did some preaching at the Methodist church attended by the Wetherills, recounted the warning he had received from a Cortez preacher.

> Bro. Hayes you never Preached to such Congs. before in all
> your life. You have scarcely half a dozen consistent Christians out-
> side of yourselves, the rest all dance, and play cards, besides, you
> have Mountain toughs, Murderers, gamblers, drunkards, thieves,
> Saloon men and keepers XXXX. I felt surprised.

As Hayes recorded, a simple trip to the post office could be disrupted in
the small town, even in the 1890s.

> A type of Western custom. Recently, a croud of drunken Men
> on the cars comeing to Mancos. They refused to pay their fare,
> and to have a little fun, they with their revolvers shot the windows
> out of the cars. Mary [Leander's adult daughter] started to go to
> the Post Office. She had just crossed the bridge over the Mancos,
> saw men running. A drunken fellow on horseback rode through
> Blksmith shop shooting his revolver across the street & rode into
> the Saloon Shooting right and left. She didn't go to the post
> office.

Benjamin Kite Wetherill died in 1898, leaving the settlement of his estate
to Al, who, of course, had the cooperation of his brothers when needed.

BLM Anasazi Heritage Center

Al Wetherill

Al remained a bachelor until he was 37 in 1898, providing editor Kelly with plenty of opportunity for ribbing. He could not resist poking fun at the bachelor when school teachers – most often female and often by mandate unmarried – became common visitors to the cliff dwellings. Al took advantage of the opportunity, bringing damsels to dances or church when opportunities arose. Kelly was always ahead of Al, reporting pranks that had gone awry. During one particular dance Al's horse was turned loose by his "well wishers," and ran off into the dark. Through the stormy, lightning-filled night, Al followed his faithful mount. He forgot his date for the evening, leaving her sitting on horseback, in the rain, in the dark, lightning flashes illuminating her silhouette. The lady was not pleased, at least according to Kelly, who described the August 1893 event in his journal.

There is no doubt but that "Al" Wetherill is one of the most accomplished and competent mountain and valley guides in the State, and one in whom we place the most implicit confidence upon extraordinary occasions. He is young, active, rather good looking (a bald head is no contradiction of this statement, if you please) an excellent conversationalist and, all in all, is an ideal guide for the numerous and enthusiastic lady visitants to the ancient cliff dwellings in the Rio Mancos Canon. His opportunities of making flattering impressions upon the minds of many fair maidens are numerous, and he makes the most of every fleeting moment, but there are times in which "Al" does not shine with extra brilliancy. Last week he had the gratification of escorting two handsome and intelligent Philadelphia ladies to the ruins, returning Saturday. On Sunday evening he saddled up two of his best horses and persuaded Miss Elizabeth, the youngest, but to our notion, not the handsomest, of the two ladies to accompany him to church....Some wretch had loosed Al's horse, and he got rattled. He put the young lady on her restive animal and skipped into the brush after his own. Here was a predicament. In a strange country, dark as possible for a night to be. Vivid flashes of lightning in the western horizon lit up the sky only to make it darker still, and then mischievous boys added to the lady's terror by yelling at her prancing horse, but her cavalier came not....

"Al's" brother John added to his discomfit by informing him that he must hereafter take along a set of cow-bells when he attempts to escort a lady to church.

The lady in question was no doubt Elizabeth Kite who so eloquently wrote of her experiences at the Alamo Ranch (see Clayton Wetherill chapter).

Al eventually was cornered by long-time Atchison school teacher Mary Tarrant. The Tarrant and Wetherill families were well acquainted from the time they lived near each other in Atchison, Kansas. Al's first attentions to a female in the Tarrant family were towards Mary's sister Laura. While on a visit to the Alamo Ranch in 1898 Mary and 37-year-old Al renewed acquaintance. The couple married the following year, beginning a 51-year partnership.

Mary helped Al as social director of the Alamo Ranch, caretaker for his mother, and Mesa Verde guide. On one such adventure she nearly lost a thumb leading a horse off a hazardous trail to the cliff dwellings. Their first tragedy was the loss of a child who died shortly after birth. Mary brought with her fine furniture and literature from Atchison. She added classics to the already burgeoning library of the Alamo Ranch – a library that after years and miles was still intact until the year 2000. A few of those books are now at the Anasazi Heritage Center; others are owned by Harvey Leake, great-grandson of John Wetherill. The rest were sold.

Fred Blackburn Collection/courtesy of Laverne Kennedy

Sterl Price Thomas

Mary was a good partner for Al but somewhat set in her ways. Missing the more cultured life of Atchison, she kept in touch with her Aunt Stella on the latest gossip and doings. She frequently traveled east to visit lifelong friends and family, later sending her child to school there. Mary never really adapted to the West and the Navajo Reservation. She was happier in a refined, urban social setting, but she held fast to Al. She knew a good man when she saw one.

Guiding was so in demand by 1898 that Al Wetherill could no longer handle the numbers. He joined marketing forces with C.E. Lewis, booking trips from the railhead in Mancos to Mesa Verde. With his brothers gone, Al linked up with livery man C.B. Kelly from Mancos and entrepreneur Sterl Thomas from Cortez, each attempting to gain a foothold in the growing tourism industry. One summer more than 250 school teachers scheduled visits to Cliff Palace, requiring the equine resources of the entire Montezuma Valley and all the resources of Wetherill, Kelly, and Thomas together to accommodate them.

Al and C.B. Kelly provided the transportation for Camp Science, a group of noted scientists who joined with officials of the Colorado Cliff Dwellings Association to formulate a plan for the future of Mesa Verde National Park. They ate a meal at the Alamo Ranch along the Mancos River, then were driven by Kelly and Wetherill to Camp Science, which was held in Soda Canyon close to Balcony House. Among the dignitaries attending the conference were Virginia McClurg, Mrs. W.S. Lucy Peabody, and special correspondent from the *New York Herald* Mrs. J.P. Maule. The visit was organized by Jesse Walter Fewkes, who later would excavate Cliff Palace and Spruce Tree House in 1908 and 1909. Fewkes spent little if any time interviewing the Wetherill family, barely mentioning them in his reports, let alone recording their observations or discoveries.

Fewkes had a second opportunity to learn about the discoveries of the Wetherills while excavating at Cliff Palace and Spruce Tree House. He chose instead to rely upon information provided by James Frink, a Mancos resident who explored the main fork of Mancos Canyon early in 1881. Frink left his carved inscriptions with other Mancos residents on a door slab below Sixteen Window House in the present-day Ute Mountain Ute Tribal Park. Frink claimed credit for the discovery of Cliff Palace as well, but according to some sources recanted his claim on his deathbed. The "Cliff Palace" Frink was referring to was more than likely Sixteen Window House. Holmes and now Fewkes both chose to ignore information from the Wetherill family.

Al joined the Cliff Dwellings Association after Camp Science, showing his support for the preservation of Mesa Verde. He understood change was coming. Adding to his dilemma of escalating guiding and ranching duties, was a wife who recently had lost a child and wished for improved social atmosphere. Their ranch was severely in debt. He was the last man standing at the Alamo.

Al and Mary chose to move from the Alamo Ranch in 1902. With his immediate family gone and the ranch in debt, Al decided to establish a trading post at Thoreau, New Mexico, east of Gallup and

BLM Anasazi Heritage Center

Fred Hyde ca. 1890

south of Richard's Chaco Canyon enterprise. Richard very likely assisted Al with inventory and initial setup. Later generations of the Wetherill family blamed Al for mismanagement and loss of the Alamo Ranch. But he had little choice in making what must have been an extremely difficult decision. Few know that Al held in his back pocket two checks. John Hayes Hammond, a man of means from London, England, who was a mining investor, evaluator, and purchaser of properties including the Smuggler Mine in Telluride, gave Al a check in 1901 to cover his debts. Hammond was a frequent visitor and supporter of the Wetherill Ranch. He understood the ranch's value and put pen to paper to ensure the Wetherills could retain it.

A second offer to pay the debts of the Alamo Ranch came from Fred and Benny Talbot Babbit Hyde, who were being encouraged by the town of Mancos to establish another of their Hyde Exploring Expedition Trading Posts in the Mancos Valley. Likely their motivation was to turn the Alamo Ranch into a trading post, which Al could not abide. After carrying Hammond's check for over a year, Al returned it to the writer, sealing the end of Wetherill family settlement along the Mancos River. There is no record of why he rejected the help, but with his brothers gone and no children to carry on the work of the ranch or guiding, Al must have felt he had no other choice but to leave. By the time Prudden published the report of his expedition with the Wetherills, the family had spread to the four winds. The days of exploration were over. Al and Mary moved on to life's new hardships.

Al's story, like those of his brothers Richard and John, is a sad one. Left out of the National Park Service's official version of the "discovery" of Cliff Palace, Al lost all credibility in officials' eyes. Edwin S. Hogg composed an article for *Touring Topics* magazine in February of 1931 after interviewing Al in Oklahoma. Among several gross inconsistencies, Hogg used literary license to put Al Wetherill in place of Charlie Mason at the discovery of Cliff Palace rather than recounting Al's earlier sighting of it in 1885.

Simultaneously and coincidentally, Mesa Verde National Park was attempting through the efforts of Jesse Nusbaum and head interpreter Don Watson to standardize the information given to visitors at Mesa Verde. One aspect of that effort was to resolve who discovered Cliff Palace. Nusbaum reviewed a copy of the Hogg article and rather than question Hogg's accuracy, deemed Al untruthful because of the inaccuracies the story contained. He told Watson that Al lacked the credibility to be taken seriously because his account conflicted with his brother John's. Given a choice, Nusbaum believed John. He and Watson made no effort to contact Al regarding the discrepancy. Al made a paragraph of notes in his journal stating his disappointment at Hogg's gross errors in the magazine article, yet made no attempt to correct them with Mesa Verde.

For the rest of his life, Al remained hurt by the misrepresentation. His daughter Martha Wetherill Stewart took up the figurative lance after Al's last visit to Mesa Verde in an attempt to correct National Park Service misconceptions and misinformation. Yet in her campaign frustration overcame communication with management staff who did not wish to listen to the stories of this gentle, humorous Quaker man. Martha's attempts to settle the story of the discovery of Cliff Palace and Al's role in it generated a voluminous exchange of correspondence between her and the National Park Service yet reached no accurate resolution. The Wetherill Family Archives contain a file termed the "War with Mesa Verde" that is filled with such letters.

Nusbaum responded to the charges brought forward by Al's daughter in June of 1945, in a short letter to Arthur E. Demaray, associate National Park Service director, addressing the 14 years of miscommunication and his take on the matter. Hogg's 1931 article had been recently reprinted in *Desert Magazine,* once again fueling the ongoing controversy. The article spurred Nusbaum into action.

> In the May issue of *Desert Magazine,* Alfred Wetherill, brother of John Wetherill and last of the five brothers who commercially exploited Mesa Verde, Chaco Canyon, and other of the major archaeological areas of the Southwest from the late 1880s, claims to have discovered, but not entered Cliff Palace in 1887 [Actually 1885] – a year in advance of our present published date of December 16, 1888, when Richard Wetherill and his brother-in-law say they discovered it and named it.

Al was further driven to complete his memoirs after his last visit to Mesa

Al Wetherill at the chief ranger house at Mesa Verde National Park.
This was Al's last visit to Mesa Verde. He was 84 years old.

THE NATIONAL PARK
AND THE WETHERILLS

Over the years, as new evidence comes to light, the National Park Service (NPS) integrates this information into the interpretive story it presents to the public. Sometimes this new evidence can lead to a complete revision of the story itself. Such has been the case with the Wetherill story and Mesa Verde National Park.

The NPS obtains the information it presents to the public from the professional community. Professional archaeologists at the beginning of the 20th century were striving for legitimacy as they established their new field. In doing so, they fought with antiquarians and amateurs to earn a respectable place in the "academy." One casualty of this conflict was the Wetherill name. Archaeologists criticized the Wetherills before Congress in the debate over the Antiquities Act. Jesse Fewkes, who headed the Bureau of American Ethnology and stabilized Cliff Palace, castigated "those who had dug into it" for wrenching "beams from the roofs and floors to use for firewood" despite a lack of evidence. Edgar Hewett, the first director of the School of American Archeology and Nusbaum's mentor, was instrumental in convincing the government to investigate Richard Wetherill's work at Chaco Canyon – an investigation that ended Wetherill's archaeological work at Pueblo Bonito.

In the early years of the National Park Service, the opinions of these early archaeologists carried a great deal of weight. As a result, rangers at Mesa Verde commonly spoke disparagingly of the Wetherill family. When Nusbaum became park superintendent, vandalism and theft of Mesa Verde's antiquities made him wary of the local populace. The Mesa Verde staff he trained, like Don Watson, inherited his critical appraisal of the Wetherills.

About mid-century, this story started to change. Nusbaum himself changed his opinion after meeting and corresponding with John Wetherill. Watson accompanied Charlie Mason, and later John, as they toured Mesa Verde and apparently revised his assessment of them as well. However, old stories die hard and as late as 1988, the chief of research at Mesa Verde criticized the Wetherill family in a public symposium.

Prior to this symposium, the NPS was already incorporating a different picture of the Wetherills due to recent scholarship. Linda Martin, the supervisory ranger for Chapin Mesa, recalls teaching rangers as early as 1976 that the Wetherills practiced archaeology as well as anyone did during their time. In 1987, David Harrell, in the *New Mexico Historical Review*, presented evidence supporting the Wetherill claims that they had tried to contact the Smithsonian. In *Ruins and Rivals* (2001), James Snead told the story of conflict that enveloped the Wetherills and early archaeologists.

Today, rangers tell visitors the Wetherill period was an important time in park history and the family did its best to preserve and protect the land they loved. Rangers often discuss the difficulties of 19th century archaeology and try to portray a complex history, one in which the Wetherill name is remembered with respect.

– Joseph Owen Weixelman, Ph.D.

**Al and John Wetherill near their camp at Johnson Canyon in 1891.
This photograph is by Gustaf Nordenskiöld.**

Verde in 1946 where he heard firsthand the defamation of his family. His grandson Tom recorded the visible shock to him.

> Al did not return to Mesa Verde until 1946, when my older brother Donald and I took our frail 84-year-old "Pop" back along the trails of his younger days. We had heard many stories from friends and relatives returning from trips to Mesa Verde with tales about the early explorers of Mesa Verde: "They had demolished the ruins. They had used dynamite to open them up. They had sold relics for tremendous sums of money." Pop resolved to return there to hear the talks himself. We took him and we heard the tales. We could see Pop's face turn pale and his eyes change from steel blue to opaque gray as he heard, "In 1888 two cowhands, Richard Wetherill and his cousin, Charles Mason discovered Cliff Palace," the Park Guide said. "That date marks the beginning of the sad history of the Mesa Verde ruins...those cowboys almost completely rifled the contents of all the ruins in Mesa Verde." I asked Pop to "set um straight," "It's no use to tell them," Pop said, "Nobody'll hear what he doesn't want to believe. I've heard what I thought I would hear."

The incident compelled Al to dust off his 1905 L.C. Smith typewriter and record for all his version of the discoveries in Mesa Verde. He typed feverishly for the next four years until his death, producing a rough draft of a book from his copious notes. The notes eventually were edited and published by Maureen Fletcher. Her book, *The Wetherills of the Mesa Verde: Autobiography of Benjamin Alfred Wetherill,* was banned from sale at Mesa Verde National Park. Criticism of the park through the park service's own correspondence in the matter was deemed not acceptable for public consumption. The family never received a cent in royalty or payment for the publication. Until recently, Al's and his family's records have been largely ignored as a result of the unfortunate interview with Hogg. The family didn't take issue with Hogg's article because they had recognized Al's story of only *viewing* the structure in 1885 and overlooked the rest. Charlie Mason acknowledged in the *Denver Post* in 1917 that Al had seen Cliff Palace first.

> About the year 1885 the Wetherill boys began to winter their cattle in the Mancos canon and its numerous branches…Richard and Al Wetherill were in this camp a greater part of each winter, Al spending more time there [than] any one else …
>   A year or more before this [referring to his and Richard's viewing] Al had seen Cliff Palace, but did not enter it; he was on his way to camp after a long tramp on foot, and was very tired; he was following the bottom of the canon and only got a partial view, so did not climb up, and it remained for Richard and I to be the first to explore the building.

Al filled at least six journals in his later years, describing in detail the family's experiences at the Alamo Ranch. Written in the late 1930s through 1950, many of the dates are off by a few years, but what he wrote was accurate if cross-checked with other sources, even if the specific dates were not. Al was scrupulously honest throughout his life. It was not in his makeup to bend a story to fit the truth. The lessons of his early Quaker upbringing resided in his character until his death.

Al was an eyewitness to drastic change occurring to prehistoric dwellings of the Mesa Verde between 1880 and 1902 when he and his family gave up on the Alamo Ranch. Al and his wife Mary maintained records and Alamo Ranch hospitality until their departure.

After decades without seeing one another, Al Wetherill and his brother-in-law Charlie Mason met for the last time near Tulsa, Oklahoma, in 1935. Al's daughter Martha was there.

> There was a brief re-union of two men this week, in Sand Springs that wasn't important enough to be listed even in the "local happenings" but because you get your stories from the little

Al Wetherill and Mary Tarrant Wetherill in Sand Springs, Oklahoma, ca. 1950.

episodes that make up the heart of humanity, instead of the big stories that "crash" the headlines, I wondered if maybe you would be interested...

It was a long story but a happy one. They were more than cattlemen. They were dreamers, and students with more than a good working knowledge of vanished races, and they loved doing it all, and giving to the world the results of their labor...

A long wait of twenty years terminated just this week when Charles Mason with his family came to see this part of the Wetherill family.

For three days, old dreams and memories lived again. But dreams fade, and memories must give way to realities, and modern living has little time for its gardens of yesterday. When the parting came again, we stood around exchanging the customary good-byes, and Al Wetherill and Charlie Mason shook hands and saw in each others' eyes a longing for the days that had been.

"Then – Well, Old Timer – I guess we'll never camp and prospect around again, to-gether."

"No, Al, I – guess – not."

Another hand clasp brief and hard...The two men smiled a little. Twenty years! The old frontiers are gone: The old pioneers are going. – and sundown must lead to night fall.

Al's brother-in-law died the following year, followed by his brother Win in 1939, and his brother John in 1944. Al outlived the last of his siblings by six years, dying in 1950 at the age of 88.

ANNA WETHERILL
& CHARLIE MASON

THE CARETAKER
AND THE FISHERMAN

Anna Isabel Wetherill

A nna Isabel Wetherill was born at Diamond Island, Kansas, on January 24, 1865, the only surviving daughter of B.K. and Marian Wetherill. Anna was the unsung hero of the Wetherill family. Charlie Mason was born in Jonesville, Wisconsin, on November 25, 1859.

Charlie and Anna's relationship began in 1877 in Joplin, Missouri, where B.K. had taken his family so he could work in the lead mines. Charlie delivered spring water to the Wetherills. Anna was 12, Charlie 18. Their attraction was instant; Anna soon announced to her parents that as soon as she turned 20 she would marry Charlie. Her promise held true, and the couple married in 1885 at the Alamo Ranch.

Charlie's father David, who was originally from Wisconsin, had moved to Joplin, then on to Pueblo, Colorado, and Mancos. He stayed only a short time in Mancos before moving first to Gallup, New Mexico, and then Corpus Christi, Texas. He eventually settled and spent the remainder of his days in Hughes Springs, Texas. When his father and family moved on, Charlie stayed behind in Mancos, working for the Wetherill family and others for as much as $1 a day.

Among other things, Charlie was the Alamo Ranch taxidermist. He enjoyed processing and mounting various animals they encountered in their travels. His mounts were displayed along with artifacts in the Alamo Ranch museum. Some were sent to Gustaf Nordenskiöld.

Charlie was a salt-of-the-earth guy, a large man with a warm smile and an obvious love for children. Anna's marriage to Charlie Mason in 1885 did not end her ranch chores. In fact, more were added with the birth of five girls while the family remained there. After their move to Hermit Lakes west of Creede they adopted three boys.

Charlie tended to chores around the Alamo and Mancos, eventually raising enough money for his own team of horses, which he named Prince and Frank. If something came up, Charlie was there to fix it. He had other assigned duties, often helping his brothers-in-law with archaeological excavation and exploration.

Anna was a tough-minded pioneer woman to have survived the confinement and hard work required of her gender in that era. Gender-related work requirements of the late 19th century dictated a division of labor. With rare exception, men did construction, field work, cowboying, and –

in the case of the Wetherill Family – exploration and excavation of the cliff dwellings. Anna's role was that of caregiver, housekeeper and cook. Regardless, B.K. and Marian Wetherill saw to a quality education for Anna.

Education within Quaker society crosses gender boundaries. Surviving letters from Anna are well written, with proper expression of thought, language and grammar. Anna's life undoubtedly was full and hard considering the number of guests, employees, and family members who inhabited the Alamo Ranch. Anna often commented on how unappreciated her role seemed to be in all the work needed to keep the household running. All household chores took hours by hand, without the conveniences of electrical or gas stoves, dishwashers, or washing machines and dryers. Days must have dragged on when washing dishes and bedding along with continually preparing meals for all field hands, visitors, brothers, husbands, and children. Anna is not known to have written any stories about the people she met sitting around the table of the Alamo Ranch, of the tales they told, or the personalities that graced the homestead. Her daughter Luella Dunkleberger, who was born at the ranch, recalled her mother telling her that people were welcome there and were encouraged to bring other "notables."

> The ranch was a place where food and lodging were acceptable to the most fastidious tastes. Everyone enjoyed the delicious dinners prepared, the homemade bread, the pie and roast cooked to a T, as Grandma would say and the freshness of each room.

Unlike the Wetherill brothers, Charlie did not develop a clientele of his own. He had other directions he wished to travel, but he believed strongly in the work his brothers-in-law did, and became a staunch defender of them. Seven years after Richard's death, Charlie initiated an affidavit of authenticity along with surviving Wetherill brothers, documenting their version of the circumstances behind their collecting in Mesa Verde. He, along with the surviving brothers, sent the signed affidavit to the Colorado Historical Society in an attempt to explain the discovery of Cliff Palace. They also wanted to speak with one voice in an effort to clear the family name and clarify their work in early exploration of Mesa Verde. Charlie's document, published in 1917 in the *Denver Post,* acknowledged Al's earlier sighting of Cliff Palace while offering yet another version of its discovery.

According to Charlie, they followed an Indian trail across Chapin Mesa between Cliff and Navajo canyons. He made no mention of Acowitz being with them, as Marietta reported in 1950. They camped at the head of a small branch of the Cliff Palace fork of Cliff Canyon, where they found a good spring under the rimrock. Near their camp was the archaeological site now known as Sun Temple, which was later excavated and reconstructed by Jesse Fewkes. Charlie and Richard's first view of the mesa top site was a large mound of rubble encased in sagebrush with a forest canopy of pinyon

Charlie Mason and his grandson's first fish.

and juniper. Near Sun Temple they found a smooth rock full of pecked concentric circles. From this location they sighted Cliff Palace across the canyon.

> To me this is the grandest view of all among Ancient Ruins of the Southwest…

In Charlie's account, he and Richard utilized lariats, logs, and prehistoric stone steps to work their way down one side of the canyon and then back up the other into Cliff Palace. Upon arrival they began a brief perusal and survey of the dwelling and contents left by the prior inhabitants. They made no indication that someone else had arrived ahead of them.

> …We spent several hours going from room to room, and picked up several articles of interest: among them a stone ax with the handle still on it. There was also parts of several human skeletons scattered about…
>
> …In the entire building only two timbers were found by us. All of the joists on which floors and roofs were laid had been wrenched out, these timbers are built into the walls and are difficult to remove: even the little willows on which the mud roofs and upper floors are laid, were carefully taken out. No plausible reason for this has been advanced except that it may have been used for fuel. Another strange circumstance is that so many of their valuable possessions were left in the room, and covered with the clay of which the roofs and upper floors were made, not to mention many of the walls that were broken down in tearing out the timbers. It would seem that their intention was to conceal their valuables so that their enemies might not secure them; or perhaps the people were in such despair that property was not considered. There were many human bones scattered about as though several people had been killed and left unburied. Had Cliff Palace been abandoned as has been suggested, and the timbers used in other buildings, all movable articles of value would have been taken instead of being covered, and much of it broken and destroyed unnecessarily…
>
> In Cliff Palace no roof beams were found. In the back were a number of scattered ~~bones~~ skeletons that had evidently not been buried. In the bottom of one Kiva was found a huge skull under six feet of debris. In the bottom of the adjoining kiva, also under debris, was found the lower jaw that fitted it. They were so large that there was no mistaking the matching.

Charlie mentioned the excavation of Spruce Tree House, Cliff Palace and Balcony House, noting that in the winter of 1889-90, after completing

Charlie Mason's photo of Keet Seel ca. 1910.

work in the Johnson Canyon area, Richard, his brothers and Charlie moved back across the Mancos River. He wrote that all the houses had been named the year before, and with completion of their excavations of these sites to their satisfaction, they were at the end of the then known cliff dwellings.

Charlie was likely involved in most of the Wetherills' collecting expeditions. A steady, dependable, hard worker, he could be relied on to complete a task. He accompanied Richard Wetherill on his 1897 expedition to Grand Gulch and to the canyons of the Tsegi at Keet Seel. Charlie returned to Kayenta, Arizona, on a visit with his family in 1910. Guided by Anna's brother John, he photographed – with a large-format, wide-angle camera – some of the earliest views of Keet Seel.

Later, as B.K.'s health deteriorated, Anna – who loved her father deeply – and Marian took responsibility for his long-term care. She read to him as his kidneys failed, noting that even when B.K. seemed not to be listening she dared not make a mistake in pronunciation of a word for he would correct her.

After B.K.'s death in 1898, Charlie and Anna's daughter Debbie stayed at the Alamo to help her grandmother. Charlie and Anna began a transition to Clear Creek, on the upper reaches of the Rio Grande River, in Mineral County, Colorado, where Charlie and Clayton finished building log cabins for the Masons in 1899. Charlie was a hard worker who often complained of being on the wrong side of the mountain, and named the area Hermit Lakes because he felt that was where he was most of the time. As he prepared for their move, Charlie traveled back and forth across the

Skidding logs for Charlie Mason, Hermit Lakes.

Continental Divide following the Weminuche Trail down the Pine River to the San Juan River at Pagosa Springs. Spring thaw and autumn snowfall made his travel through the high mountain Weminuche Pass particularly difficult. Charlie and Anna struggled for survival in that first year. Perched at an elevation of 10,000 feet, life at Hermit Lakes was harder than it had been in Mancos. Charlie cowboyed for Bert Hosselkus, who helped him establish commercial trout fisheries. Marian Wetherill wrote Anna that she would send them money if she could but they did not have things in money, "only in food and comfort." She advised that the relics would soon sell and they could forward money to help them out. She also suggested selling the horses if need be to make it through the winter.

Charlie's Mancos friendships had led him not only to the Creede area, but to the work he would do there. He considered Wash Patrick, Charles McLoyd, and J.H. Graham friends. From Patrick and Graham, he would have learned about the Pine River, since they had well-established roots along the Pine on the west side of the Continental Divide. Charlie would have had ample time to talk with Patrick during their excavation of Cliff Palace. During these conversations Charlie was likely taken by the possibility of raising fish. There is little doubt that Patrick was his mentor. The man was fascinated with fish. He built the first fish hatcheries in Durango and created a hatchery at Vallecito using Emerald and Flint lakes for breeding (lakes whose names were vibrantly chosen in naming his son, Emerald Flint Patrick). Patrick became the first fish commissioner for the state of Colorado and later helped actor Noah Berry with a hatchery in the Sierras. Undoubtedly Charlie's relationship with Patrick influenced his decision to create similar hatcheries in South Clear Creek. Railroad at hand, he imported eastern brook trout, raised them to a correct size, then shipped them to market by rail from the mining town of

Charlie Mason ca. 1930.

The Mason homestead at Hermit Lakes, Anna is standing in the doorway.

Creede. Charlie Mason was granted the first commercial license by the United States government for the culture and sale of trout.

With Charlie and Anna gone, along with Clayton, Al was the only Wetherill man remaining to oversee the Alamo Ranch. During the spring of 1899 Debbie Mason and her grandmother moved to live with Charlie and Anna and their family. Marian took with her letters, photos, diaries, and other family papers from her early years with B.K. Sadly, many of them were lost over the years in two house fires and a theft. With Anna's heart wearing out, Charlie and the family chose to move from Hermit Lakes to a lower coastal elevation near Rignall, Washington. Here the fish were bigger and Charlie enjoyed sport fishing for salmon while working in the oyster industry. Charlie's interests had developed beyond the fish hatchery into sport fishing. *Outdoor Life* magazine in the 1920s published a pictorial of his ventures. From a distance Charlie began selling cabin property investments and rights for exclusive sport fishing in Colorado while living in Rignall. Charles Christopher Mason died in Olympia, Washington, in January 1936. Anna Wetherill Mason died in Washington the following year. A large number of their descendants continue to live in the Olympia area.

Charlie and Anna made numerous contributions to the success of visitor service and excavations based at the Alamo Ranch. Unlike most of the Wetherill brothers who continued exploring archaeological sites elsewhere in the region after leaving the Alamo Ranch, Charlie turned his attentions to raising fish. Only Clayton Wetherill followed Charlie's lead, also establishing a fish hatchery.

JOHN WETHERILL

SOUTHWEST
ARCHAEOLOGY'S
PIONEER

Louisa and John ca. 1930.

J ohn Wetherill was born on Diamond Island near Leavenworth, Kansas, on September 24, 1866. His father B.K. may have run a sawmill on the small island in the Missouri River before a flood washed away their home and enterprise. Louisa Wade was born on September 2, 1877, in Ward City, Nevada. They were married March 17, 1896, in Mancos, Colorado.

John Wetherill, while quick-witted and well-educated, was quietly surrounded by historically notable individuals. His and his wife Louisa's advice was sought by a United States president, artists, writers, generals, archaeologists, anthropologists, and botanists. The Wetherill family experience was the garment while John and Louisa Wetherill wove the thread connecting their histories. John's lifetime of archaeological discovery spanned 60 years of pioneering in the Four Corners.

John was a quiet man who carried an aura of respect. As a guide, he chose to let his clients "discover" and take credit for much of what he and

Fred Blackburn Collection/Gustaf Nordenskiöld

John Wetherill photographed by Gustaf Nordenskiöld. The National Park Service used this photograph as the cover on an invitation to the 1992 opening of the Mesa Verde Research Library.

his life partner Louisa already knew. That may be one reason that he alone among the Wetherill brothers gained some respect from the National Park Service. Longtime Park Superintendent Jesse Nusbaum had criticized the Wetherill brothers harshly, particularly Al and Richard, for "commercially exploiting" Mesa Verde and other sites throughout the Southwest. Yet John somehow overcame such defamation and earned Nusbaum's respect. The Mesa Verde National Park superintendent even eulogized John and Louisa at the dedication of a memorial to them in Kayenta in 1954.

John wrote of the roles his brothers played in building an understanding of complex archaeological interpretations of Ancestral Puebloan people. He remained close to all his brothers and in many ways reflected traits exemplified by his father. His intimate connections to archaeology as well as to Navajo and Ute people were respected and well known beyond the archaeological community. Navajos demonstrated their respect for John when they bestowed on him the Navajo title *Hosteen* (Mr., boss, or sir) and on his wife Louisa *Asthon Sosie* (Slim Woman).

John handled conflict or accusation by lifting one side of his mouth in a quizzical grin and walking away. When questioned he would reply, "It is hard to argue with someone who is not talking!" Such a moment came on a visit with clients to Mesa Verde during the 1930s. As John visited Balcony House he was confronted with a frigid and hostile reception much as Al would receive many years later. On a ranger-guided tour, John suffered through uninformed accusations, listening to stories of how his family threw artifacts from the cliff dwelling over the edge of the cliff. Artifacts mentioned included loom poles, wooden items, and pottery – artifacts Virginia McClurg had quite clearly stated were removed in her 1886 visit. Despite his anger John forced a smile and walked away. He used the same technique at Kayenta when his nephew Kipling Wade, of Moab, came for a visit with friends. An incident of misbehavior provoked a response from John that said it all, "You better hit the road boys."

Martha Wetherill Stewart, Al's daughter, obtained another insight into the workings of John Wetherill when she asked Al in questionnaire form about a conflict with brother Win.

> Did you and Uncle Win get to the point of "words" or did Uncle John rescue you before you severed diplomatic relations?
> Al's response was: "No words we just got up and went – John want[ed] me to get up and go the minute he got in…"

BLM Anasazi Heritage Center

Louisa Wade Wetherill ca. 1923.

John's life partner was Louisa Wade. They were opposites in many ways regarding their views on life, but agreed wholeheartedly with regard to the respect and treatment due indigenous Americans. While John explored the canyons, Louisa explored language, culture, and ethnobotany of the Navajo and Ute people, whom she would attempt to assist throughout her life.

John and Louisa came from pioneering families but of different culture and geographic location. The Wetherills were from the Quaker communities of Pennsylvania and Iowa, the Wade and Rush families from Virginia, Georgia, and Texas hill country. Jenny Wade, an aunt of Louisa, was the only woman killed at the battle of Gettysburg. While she was baking bread for the battling troops a stray bullet took her life.

Louisa's grandfather, James Martin Rush Sr., was a colorful character. Born in Hambersham County, Georgia, on December 19, 1819, Rush exemplified true western life. He served as a Texas Ranger prior to 1846. War with Mexico saw Rush helping Texas with the effort. He enlisted in the Confederate Army during the Civil War, but was honorably discharged after six months so that he could take charge of a wagon train taking cotton to Monterey, Mexico, in a Confederate Army attempt to raise war

The Rush family traveling from Nevada with baby Louisa ca. 1879.

funds through commerce with Mexico. Rush's first wife and child died early. He took a second wife, Louisa Wortham, after whom their grand-daughter Louisa Wade would be named. Rush left Texas in 1866, traveling to Oregon City, Oregon, then on to California in 1869. He brought his family to Humboldt County, Nevada, in 1872, after which they moved to Mancos, traveling through "Monumental Valley" with their daughter and 3-year-old granddaughter Louisa. The Wade family settled at Mancos in 1879. Louisa's mother recorded their first experience in Monument Valley, which eventually would become John and Louisa's long-term home.

> ...we remained at Silver Reef until the third day of April 1880, and then came over the Buckskin Mountains and south to Lee's Ferry on the Colorado River and to Tuba City. This was the last place where anyone was living which we saw until we came to the San Juan River. We came across country by road. Bill Hyde had crossed the same country the year before, and we were trying to fol-low his trail. Once in a while we would see a wagon track through the sagebrush. But the Indians (Navajos) showed us the way. We were nineteen days making it from Tuba City to the San Juan. Sometimes we thought we would never get through. One place we camped on our way through the Navajo country is now known as Kayenta. My oldest daughter and her husband, John Wetherill, have a trading store there and a tourist headquarters also. She was a little girl three years old when we camped there and always remem-bered it because we had such a gorgeous sunset that night.

Louisa loved to socialize and enjoyed a good party. John, on the other hand, preferred sitting in the background quietly smoking a hand-rolled cigarette. Legs crossed, hand resting on a knee, a short cigarette dangling between two fingers of his weathered hand, John carefully observed events unfolding around him. Louisa relied heavily upon John's inner strength to sustain her through many trials. John and Louisa were immediately attracted to one another. Much of their combined accomplishments occurred long after the initial discoveries in Cliff Palace, but that is another story. They carried with them to Oljato and then Kayenta the standards for hospitality established at the Alamo Ranch, and continued to attract diverse personalities and interests.

John indicated that his first excavation after coming to Mancos occurred in 1881, between the Alamo Ranch and the town of Mancos. The rubble mound remains visible off the paved back road into the southern edge of Mancos. While he did not ever write about the family's collection of artifacts from Hemenway House 2 (Brownstone Front) in 1885, John did tell of a collection obtained in Mancos Canyon and Johnson Canyon, which the family sold to Chain and Hardy in 1886 and 1887. John signed his name and the date 1887 in Sandal House possibly during the 1886-1887 gathering of that collection.

The 1888 excavation of Cliff Palace with Charles McLoyd, J.H. Graham, and Wash Patrick was later described by John in response to a query from Jesse Nusbaum.

> We had no opposition while working on the Mesa Verde. Mcloyd (Dead), Patrick and Graham worked for two months with me while we were in Cliff Palace, Spruce Tree House and Square Tower House. We named these houses at that time.

Nusbaum questioned John regarding the amount of money paid for the 1888 McLoyd collection sold to the Colorado Historical Society. He had been led to believe by other sources that they were paid $10,000 cash for the collection. John refuted the claim, stating the most money paid for any collection was $3,000, but he neglected to add that McLoyd had received that payment, *not* the Wetherill brothers. Nonetheless, the story of supposed high cash payments received by the family is a pernicious element of Mesa Verde interpretation and local legend.

John spent a great deal of his time in Spruce Tree House while excavating with McLoyd. His single inscription appears numerous times within the dwelling, potentially indicating he was working alone. One inscription is easily viewed, a deeply carved "JW" on a large boulder in the southeast portion of the alcove. Artifacts in Spruce Tree House were very limited — indicating possibly that the dwelling was thoroughly stripped by its original inhabitants before they departed.

John Wetherill's inscription at Spruce Tree House.

After these first excavations led by McLoyd, the Wetherill family was accused of utilizing dynamite in the ruins to blow holes in the walls, ostensibly to create ventilation, scare rattlesnakes, or gain access to otherwise inaccessible locations. All such accusations are lacking substance in fact, even though plaster testing in 2003 revealed traces of dynamite residue on a large kiva in the western edge of Cliff Palace.

Nusbaum had identified Jim Jarvis, a Durango/Aztec native, as the source of allegations that the Wetherills had used dynamite in cliff dwellings. Jarvis had, in fact, collaborated with the Wetherill brothers on excavations. However, when interviewed by McNitt, Jarvis flatly denied Nusbaum's claim. He said he had used some dynamite in the Aztec Ruins but never knew of any use of dynamite by the Wetherills within Mesa Verde.

A possible explanation for traces of dynamite residue lies in a drainage project. Dynamite was used in 1961 in the blasting of a drift (horizontal passageway) below and behind Cliff Palace to divert water away from the front of the dwelling, thereby hopefully avoiding slippage of the room blocks into the canyon. It was not a common practice to store dynamite in the drift to be blasted, so it might have been stored in the suspect kiva, an area dry and well away from prying hands.

Alfred Vincent Kidder addressed the dynamite accusation after working with Clayton Wetherill in Marsh Pass, Arizona.

> But, by and large, the Mesa Verde cliffhouses suffered much less vandalism than used to be said; and stories of destruction by the

HELEN "TROT" HENDERSON CHAIN

James Albert (J.A.) Chain and S.B. Hardy were booksellers and stationers in Denver, and were associated with photographer William Henry Jackson. They were familiar with Jackson's work with the 1874 and 1875 Hayden Survey parties in the Mancos Canyon. Chain's wife, Helen

BLM Anasazi Heritage Center

Henderson Chain, later proved instrumental in arranging for the 1888 McLoyd Collection sale to the Colorado Historical Society. She accompanied William Henry Jackson to the Mancos River, where both left their inscriptions in Sixteen Window House on February 23, 1889. She was a noted artist and art teacher in the Denver area.

Mrs. Chain and her husband were well known as philanthropists. Her nickname was "Trot" for all of her traveling about the globe. The couple was lost at sea in 1892 while traveling by steamer from Hong Kong to Shanghai. Their vessel was grounded on a deserted island. Twenty-three people survived the tragedy. Years later her ring was found washed up on the shore of the China Sea.

Wetherill brothers have been greatly exaggerated. Tales of their having dynamited walls that impeded their work were pure inventions. They knew too much of the danger of rocks falling from the sometimes unstable cave roofs to risk weakening them by explosions.

Dynamite is never mentioned in Wetherill family accounts of discovery or excavation. Louisa Wetherill provided a secondhand glimpse of what it was like to excavate within the ruins the winter of 1888-89.

Through that month of snow the boys lived in that high place of a ruin. With its massive tower and its two hundred rooms there seemed to them only one possible name. They called it Cliff Palace. During that time they worked also at Square Tower House and at Spruce Tree House, with its hundred and fourteen rooms and eight kivas. In the smaller ruin, closer to the floor of the cañon, there was a feeling of intimacy, unlike the great Cliff Palace. But still the treetops were below them, and in their cave they were in a silent place apart. Near Spruce Tree House some

John Wetherill at Eagle's Nest in the eventual Ute Mountain Ute Tribal Park. This photograph was taken by Frederick Chapin.

A Gustaf Nordenskiöld photograph of Al Wetherill and John Wetherill in Nordenskiöld house, Ute Mountain Ute Tribal Park.

John Wetherill in Long House, 1891. Photograph by Gustaf Nordenskiöld.

1891 Gustaf Nordenskiöld photograph of John at Cliff Palace.

smaller houses clung to a high ledge that seemed at first inaccessible. But at the head of the cañon, John found a place to let down a pole, and sliding down, reached the level of the unexplored houses, the first into still new ruins.

John's description of their excavations at Cliff Palace and elsewhere make it clear that blasting through walls and floors played no part in their work. He also noted the possible cause of previous damage to the structure.

> The best finds we made in the Mesa Verde were in the dark cave near the head of Fewkes Canon, in Mummy Cave in Pool Canon about four miles from Cliff Palace in Step House and in Fortified House in Acowitz Canon. In Fortified House the most of the material came from the rooms. In the other ruins the material came mostly from dry sand under protecting cliffs, where there were cliff houses. It came mostly from cists. One ruin in Mountain Sheep Canon had a large number of pots laying in the ruin. In Broken Canon we found a bow, a baby board, a lot of matting, willow and rush, several baskets and a number of other articles. There was a few inches of dust in the cave. The most of the stuff was in sight.
>
> We found a large amount of material in Cliff Palace. The most

John at Balcony House. Photograph by Gustaf Nordenskiöld, 1891.

John (seated in center) taking notes at Nordenskiöld House.
Gustaf Nordenskiöld photo, 1891.

of it scattered around the rooms. Bone awls, knives, stone axes, baskets, and pottery. Almost every room paid us for working. There was from one to five feet of rubbish in each one. A large part in some of the rooms was the upper floors fallen in after the timber was removed.

The last statement by John concerning the potential of prehistoric removal of timbers from Cliff Palace is quite revealing. The timbers which McLoyd and subsequent Wetherill parties were later accused of having burned as firewood had clearly been removed before they entered the site.

John took detailed notes for Gustaf Nordenskiöld during their work in Mesa Verde. Photographs taken by Nordenskiöld often show John making notes while Gustaf photographed the prehistoric features within the alcove. Although a common practice in archaeology today, this team approach of photography and note-taking was virtually unknown in 1891. The combination of their collaboration and Nordenskiöld's talent of perseverance undoubtedly contributed greatly to the amazingly quick publication of Nordenskiöld's *The Cliff Dwellers of the Mesa Verde* in 1893.

John, Nordenskiöld, and two unnamed Hispanic workers set up a camp in 1891 on the north end of Wetherill Mesa. Water is scarce there, but a nearby spring, though not ideal, provided enough water for horse and man. They began work in Long House based on John's advice. Nordenskiöld credited John with identifying improvised tombs found

Artifact discovery 1891. Photographed by Gustaf Nordenskiöld.

within the cliff dwellings, recounting a story of John's discovery of a very old man in a crypt burial with a single bowl.

Nordenskiöld went on to quote John's notes about the discovery of another most unusual burial during Wetherill family excavations in 1890 and 1891 in Johnson Canyon. John's descriptions once again reflect his skills in both observing and writing, at the same time also noting previous 1883 excavations at the site by Captain Baker of Fort Lewis.

> We (Charley Mason and John Wetherill) dug a while in a room we had worked in before dinner; but finding nothing I began shoveling in a room Captain Baker's men had nearly cleared. Glancing up I noticed a door that had been sealed up. I removed a rock and saw that it was the only entrance. I told Charley of this, and he said I would find a skeleton. I removed the rocks down to the floor and noticed some wrappings, the same that they bury the dead in. While clearing away the rubbish I found a piece of a cinch. It was three-coloured, red, white and black. I then broke through the wall [the sealed door mentioned above] on another side. As soon as I dug to the floor I uncovered more matting. I removed some dirt and found an arrow with an agate point on it,

the first ever found in a Cliff-house in Mancos Canon. I took it to where Charley was, and he concluded to help me dig. Charley removed two or three shovelfuls of dirt and dug out a basket; it was 12 inches across the top and 6 inches deep. Henceforward our finds came fast and close together. We found 17 arrows lying across the heads of five bodies. Between the skulls were four bowls. One large skeleton lay on the top of the mat with bow on one side, a mug and a basket on the other. He had nothing over him; a pair of moccasins on his feet and some feather cloth under his head. Near him lay a hollow stick with both ends wrapped with sinew and with a bone-point at the end about six inches long. The stick was about twenty inches long. Lying alongside of this body were the skeletons of three babies. The rats had eaten them so much that they were not worth saving. Two of them had pieces of buckskin with them. After taking them up we found a large mat covering the whole floor. We removed this and found another skeleton and a stick with a loop at the end, that we took for a medicine stick, also two prairie-dog skin pouches. The skeleton was covered with a willow mat. Under the mat were two more made of grass. Under the grass mat was one of feather cloth, after that a buckskin-jacket with fringes. We found also two awls and a walnut, and in the same room two or three buckskin bags. The three baby skeletons were lying on the skeleton with the buckskin jacket. A large mug lay at the head of one of the babies. The three baby skeletons and the one on the top lay with their heads up the canon, while the other had its head down the canon.

Gustaf Nordenskiöld and John Wetherill forged a symbiotic relationship often ignored by the National Park Service in exhibits and interpretation. A photograph of John taken by Nordenskiöld appeared as the front cover for an invitation to the opening of the Mesa Verde Research Library on May 14, 1992, yet John was not identified. Instead the National Park Service has described Nordenskiöld as sole designer of the first scientific excavation in Mesa Verde National Park. The Swede did teach John, and subsequently his brothers, the value of stratigraphy as well as a scientific approach to cataloguing and mapping. It was just the kind of guidance B.K. had sought for his family from the Smithsonian, and been refused by archaeologist William H. Holmes.

John noted his observations of stratigraphy when recounting discovery of mica pottery in Step House on Wetherill Mesa while excavating with Nordenskiöld. He found a large pottery "tray" four and one-half feet deep, below the remains of the later Pueblo occupation. He noted that these early attempts at pottery making had been done by people who already had well-developed basketry – people who later were designated

Basketmaker III. At the time, John believed that Nordenskiöld, along with his brothers, did not understand they had found remnants from an earlier cultural group who predated the cliff dwelling builders.

What Nordenskiöld taught the Wetherill brothers is best demonstrated in their improved documentation of Basketmaker and Puebloan discoveries during later expeditions. In return, John – and to a limited extent his brothers – provided Nordenskiöld with detailed notes and subtle observations and keen understanding of the Ancestral Puebloans. John, as well as his brothers, recognized the existence of many subcultural groups among the people then known as the Cliff Dwellers. John explained their place in time.

Fred Blackburn Collection

D.W. and Marie Ayres ca. 1860.

The name Cliff Dweller is a name given to a people who lived under the cliffs in parts of Colorado, New Mexico, Arizona and Utah and even down in Old Mexico. They are generally supposed to be one people or tribe, but they are many tribes with similar habits and modes of living...

Without the mutually beneficial relationship formed with Nordenskiöld, the Wetherills would not have understood the implications of their findings at Basketmaker sites. Al's previously described excavation from 1893 following charcoal soil staining into the burials of Cave 7 in southeastern Utah was a direct result of what John had learned from Nordenskiöld and in turn taught him and Richard.

John was in charge of the collection for the state of Colorado exhibit at the World's Columbian Exposition. Along with D.W. Ayres, he assembled a collection for A.F. Willmarth in 1892. John also worked with his brothers in compiling additional materials for H. Jay Smith's Battle Rock Mountain exhibit at the same exposition. Two simultaneous excavations were underway in Mesa Verde in a great race to accumulate artifacts for display. John described the assignment to Jesse Nusbaum in a letter ca. 1940.

I had charge of the field work for the State collection for the Chicago Fair. At that time there were no American Archeologist[s] in the field. We tried often to get them interested but they would not come.

Referring to his 1892 work within Mesa Verde, John suggested to Nusbaum that the American archaeological community only became interested in southwestern work around the time Nusbaum began work on Balcony House in 1910.

Al, Charlie Mason, and John returned to Step House in 1892 to add to their existing collection for Smith's Battle Rock Mountain exhibit. John described this collection in detail and elaborated on additional mica pottery discoveries within Step House. He also detailed an account of an earlier structure built by the Ancestral Puebloans now known as a pithouse.

> I began working where I had found the tray and uncovered the bottom of a room about 8 x 10 feet. The walls had been about 1½ feet high and posts had been set in the corners of the room and had been burned off even with the top of the wall. The upper part of the room had been built of timber and all been destroyed by fire. We found twenty-four pieces besides the one that Nordenskjold [sic] had taken. There was no other piece with any sort of design on it. The pottery was all rough but it glistened with mica. The pieces were mostly of the same shape much like the pitchers of the Cliff Dwellers except that they had no handles. We found no skeletons, baskets, bone tools, sandals, no indications that they farmed or raised turkeys.

> The amount of data was so limited that about the only things we had to go on was the way the rooms were built and the great difference in pottery...

John's findings in Step House were followed by a second observation while he and Al accompanied Charles McLoyd into Grand Gulch during the winter of 1892. McLoyd had gathered a collection of human skulls he termed Cliff Dweller but John noted a difference. One of the skulls in McLoyd's collection showed no evidence of skull deformation caused from cradle boards.

> I saw at once that they had something different from anything I had ever seen from the cliffs. Tho they had quite a lot of the regular cliff dweller relics. I asked them what they had and they said they didn't know. They gave us a skull which we took home. Prof Workman at that time from Cornell saw it and once proclaimed it an Apache...

Although the Apache identification was incorrect, John's recognition of the distinctive skull characteristics was accurate and became an important turning point. Searching for an explanation, he had once again turned to a

EXPERIENCING HRDLICKA

In 1899 and 1900 John guided Ales Hrdlicka renowned anthropologist of his time, on an extended tour through the West. This was perhaps the most challenging of all of John's guiding. Louisa missed him terribly during his extended absence. Their newborn child Georgia Ida and the distance apart proved hard for newlywed Louisa. John and Hrdlicka covered 2,500 miles by team and wagon or horse and packhorse. Their journeys took them deep into ethnological studies and some excavation at Fort Apache, San Carlos, Hopi villages, and Laguna and Acoma pueblos. They also excavated in McElmo Canyon near Cortez and Allen Canyon near present-day Blanding, Utah. Louisa's letters to John allude to his discontent with Hrdlicka, a Czech anthropologist who had developed theories regarding Asian migration across the frozen Bering Strait during the Ice Age. Hrdlicka based his premise on the ancient projectile points found far to the north.

Not surprisingly, in that era of Manifest Destiny when it was popularly believed that intelligence could be determined by skull size (and hence, brain capacity), Hrdlicka was very interested in the measurement and collection of skulls. Years after his visit to Mancos, Al summed up the family experience with Hrdlicka in a wry comment about an article on the Czech anthropologist's life. According to the Czech scientist, Al said, "My arms were too long, my legs too short and my head too big but other than that I was a perfect physical specimen." The idea of a superior physical and mental "type" was completely contrary to everything Al and the family believed as Quakers.

known professor of the time, valuing the knowledge and opinions of others more educated in the field than he. Combined with solid evidence from their excavations in Cave 7 and Grand Gulch during the 1893 and 1894 Hyde Exploring Expedition, John and his brothers believed they were indeed looking at a distinct earlier occupation of people. Based on their findings, they suggested that their benefactors name these earlier people Basketmakers.

Many years later, John and his brother Clayton helped Samuel Guernsey, Alfred Vincent Kidder, and others from the Peabody Museum of Harvard University in 1914-1917 to excavate in the Marsh Pass area in northeastern Arizona. The brothers shared the conclusion they'd drawn from their earlier discoveries regarding the Basketmakers. To John, the fact that Kidder and Guernsey recognized the same patterns Richard had identified nearly 25 years before was a vindication of his family.

> The first year Dr. Guernsey worked the evidence was not conclusive enough to make it an actual fact, but the second year he found enough evidence to prove that they did exist for the south side of the San Juan and that they were beyond a doubt a separate ~~people~~

tribe. He found no evidence that they lived under the cliffs only that they buried there and had their extra surplus cached things.

In the late 1930s John wrote less than 15 pages – all in pencil – likely at the request of Jesse Nusbaum, to explain nearly 60 years of archaeological observations. Much of the writing is devoted to an explanation of the kiva and its variations in construction, and dissimilarities between the Basketmaker, Valley and Cliff Dwellers.

John Wetherill was very supportive of Jesse Nusbaum's work in Mesa Verde National Park. Although Nusbaum's reciprocated interest in John is suspect in light of some of his later writings, the two maintained an amiable relationship in their correspondence. Nusbaum's first connection to John likely occurred in 1934 when Nusbaum told him about John D. Rockefeller's contributions to funding the infrastructure of Mesa Verde National Park. He provided John with a letter of introduction for the Rockefellers' visit to Kayenta.

> It is always a worthy act to bring mutual friends together and I wish it might be my pleasure to personally introduce Mr. John D. Rockefeller Jr. and his son David to the Wetherills.

John wrote a letter to Nusbaum in June of 1936 asking that his nephew Jack Wade be rehired by the park, expressing enthusiasm for Nusbaum's return to the park as superintendent.

> Mrs. Wetherill and I are glad to know that you are in charge again. I will try and see you some time this summer. We both wish you and your wife the best that can be had.

Nusbaum in 1944 relied on John when he wished to present a case for the reintroduction of mountain sheep into the region of the Mesa Verde. Two months before his death, John wrote an explanation to Nusbaum and Jack Wade of encounters both historic and prehistoric with mountain sheep while he and Gustaf Nordenskiöld excavated on Wetherill Mesa.

> …he and I were about to enter Long House on the Wetherill Mesa, when a bighorn came charging through the trees and stopped within forty-five feet of us. He was a Rocky Mountain Bighorn. There were five of them on the Wetherill Mesa, while we were with Nordenskiöld. We ran into them several times. We found the horns of two of them in what we called Mountain Sheep Canyon. They should be in the Nordenskiöld collection…

John went on to note that they had collected pieces of sheep skin and a pair of high moccasins with hair now located at the Colorado Historical

Society in Denver. A second letter sent to his nephew Jack Wade, then acting Mesa Verde National Park chief ranger, further explained the archaeological context associated with mountain sheep. John was sure the sheep he and Nordenskiöld observed were Rocky Mountain bighorn and not desert bighorns. He provided Jack some advice.

Zeke Johnson at the Goblet of Venus ca. 1920

The way to find out about sheep is to visit the collections from the Mesa. The one in the museum in Philadelphia has a large collection and quite a bit of sheep skin. In 1889 and 90 we could see them on the Wetherill Mesa every once in a while. The tracks were most everywhere. The mesa sheep were larger than anything we ever saw in southern Arizona or Mexico. The horns we have here came from near Tule Well on the Camino Diablo between Ajo and Yuma. They measure 16 inches at the butts while Mesa Verde's measured about 18 inches, from that to 19 inches. There is not much I can tell you because we never killed any. We found the horns where the Utes had killed them.

John continued to guide and train archaeologists and anthropologists throughout the Southwest and eventually in Mexico. Neil Judd, Byron Cummings, Earl Morris, Nels C. Nelson, Frederick Ward Putnam, Alfred Vincent Kidder, Samuel Guernsey, Lyndon Hardgrave, and Edgar Hewett were but a few he helped along the way. He guided Charles Bernheimer, with the help of fellow guide Mormon Zeke Johnson, on numerous Bernheimer Expeditions. John and his son Ben aided the Rainbow Bridge Monument Valley Expedition directed by Ansel Hall. John also assisted in the excavation of Keet Seel and Betatakin with Byron Cummings. Former President Teddy Roosevelt and his family made several trips to Kayenta and one to the famous Rainbow Bridge in 1913. Yet John's only statement

President Teddy Roosevelt and John Wetherill.

to Jesse Nusbaum about the expeditions consisted of a single sentence.

> I have been out with a number of research parties ...

John Wetherill's accomplishments, along with those of his wife Louisa, could fill volumes. His friendship with Ansel Hall, photographer and organizer of the Rainbow Bridge Monument Valley Expedition of the 1930s, was long-standing. Hall – who became owner and general manager of the Mesa Verde Company, park concessionaire, in 1939 – invited John to be an instructor at Mesa Verde in 1944, sharing his experiences of the early years of exploration within the national park.

Unfortunately, by then John's heart was failing. He traveled regularly between the home of the Jim Wade family in California and his beloved home at the trading post in Kayenta. California's lower elevation helped his breathing and eased his pain. John was listed on the brochure for the Mesa Verde interpretive training in the spring of 1944, but took a turn for the worse just prior to the event. Instead of going to Mesa Verde, he boarded the train in Flagstaff and headed for California. On the train he wrote a letter to Louisa telling her that he sat with a group of black soldiers and felt that if they were good enough to fight for this country they were good enough to sit next to. It was the first time in his life that he had the opportunity to do so. West of Flagstaff at Ash Fork, Arizona, John died alone on the train. He was 78 years old. Within two years his business partner Clyde Colville, his wife Louisa, and his son Ben were also dead. Emil Haury, distinguished University of Arizona archaeologist, helped to settle their combined estates. A void was felt both in the archaeological community and among the Navajo people they had so long served.

Maude Freeland provided comments regarding John in the *Taney County Republican* of Forsythe, Missouri, summing up his character.

> John Wetherill was a comforting host. He had lived a life close to simple things and without pride he could give one a rich store of knowledge garnered in the places not known to the practiced traveler...It takes a strong character and a just one to live so long as John Wetherill lived with one group of Indians and to have kept their confidence and friendship...

John and Louisa Wetherill's deaths were too quick an end, one that Harold Colton, director of the Museum of Northern Arizona in Flagstaff, could not ignore. Colton worked hard starting in 1945 arranging for a memorial to this pioneer family at Kayenta. He compiled two publications of Louisa's life's work, one on her ethnobotanical collection and a second on her work with Kayenta Navajo sand paintings. The Navajo tribe donated two acres of land for the memorial which was dedicated in 1954. Jesse

Louisa Wade with Navajo friends at Kayenta.

Nusbaum compiled a list of expeditions completed by John, noting his many accomplishments in archaeology. Harry Dixon designed the memorial bronze plaque. Albert Bradley, a Navajo friend of the family, and son-in-law Buck Rogers completed the installation. Contributions came from the American public and the archaeological community, among them Clyde Kluckhohn, Leland C. Wyman, Horace Albright, Barry Goldwater, Herbert E. Gregory, Nels C. Nelson, Jesse L. Nusbaum, John D. Rockefeller Jr., and Stuart M. Young. Many of John's Navajo friends appeared in their best dress to pay honor to their friends.

Today the bronze plaque is pinged by hammer blows and encroachment of other development has reduced the two acres to a few feet. Tumbleweeds and trash accumulate inside and outside of the enclosure. The Kayenta Trading Post, so hard won from the desert, has been razed.

Louisa Wade Wetherill and Hoskinni Begay at Kayenta.

CLAYTON WETHERILL

THE HUMAN
PLUMB BOB

C layton Wetherill was born in March of 1868 in Atchison, Kansas. On May 7, 1907, at the age of 39, he married Eugenia Faunce, in Mancos. Eugenia was 17 years his junior and the sister of his brother Winslow's second wife, Hilda. The service was held under the guidance of D.E. Bundy, a Methodist minister. Without other Friends in the area, the Wetherill family had chosen to affiliate with the Methodist Church while continuing to practice their Quaker beliefs. Clayton's mother Marian taught Sunday School. Hilda, who was already married to Winslow Wetherill, and Ruth Wattles witnessed the wedding. On May 13, 1907, in a shallow alcove on the old route to Balcony House, Eugenia commemorated their marriage by inscribing in large letters on the sandstone alcove wall "Clayton Wetherill and Eugenia Wetherill" and the date of their honeymoon trip to Mesa Verde. It was the last inscription by a Wetherill within Mesa Verde.

BLM Anasazi Heritage Center

Clayton Wetherill as a young man.

Eugenia and Hilda's mother, Dr. Mary Ann Wattles, is of interest as well. Mary Ann attended college in Oberlin, Ohio, then studied medicine under Dr. Emily Blackwell in New York. She left New York to complete her medical degree in Germany, then returned to practice medicine in New York City while teaching anatomy at the New York Women's Medical College. She married Carroll Sylvanius Faunce, a textile mill designer in New York, on July 4, 1882. After their marriage, she continued to practice and teach medicine until 1898 when Carroll decided to move west. She received her license to practice medicine in Colorado in Fort Collins before moving on to Mancos, where they lived until 1912. Carroll returned to New York for many years while Mary Ann moved to Creede, where she lived with Clayton and Eugenia.

In 1888 when Clayton was 20 years old, he suffered an acute attack of inflammatory rheumatism, now known as rheumatic fever, while attending school in Durango. B.K. rushed to his son's bedside expressing his concern while aiding with what comfort he could provide. The next day, Richard and Charlie Mason set eyes on Cliff Palace for the first time. Meanwhile, Clayton endured a fever so severe that the illness permanently weakened

BLM Anasazi Heritage Center

Clayton Wetherill

his heart. Flirting with death may have inspired Clayton in his daredevil climbing attempts.

The following spring, young Clayton provided an artifact to a Durango museum, undoubtedly retrieved by one of his brothers from excavations the previous winter. It may have been one of Clayton's early discoveries from a rubble mound north of the Alamo Ranch, where – he told Nordenskiöld in 1891 – he had uncovered a clay pot full of beans.

Access to the ruins of the Mesa Verde was at times very difficult. Puebloan ladders that once lay against sheer unbroken rock and carved oblique footholds were gone or unusable. Explorers were innovative. Clayton, young man that he was, had a fearless streak. After tying a special quick release knot around the saddle horn, Clayt, as he was known by family, was lowered by his brothers into otherwise impossible entrances to cliff dwellings. While hanging in mid-air he would swing like a pendulum until he was close enough to grab onto a rock, tree, or architectural feature and from there get into the dwelling. Clayt's signature is often found written in charcoal in many hard-to-reach locations within the Mesa Verde. He prearranged a signal to let his brothers know he was finished with his reconnaissance or excavation and ready to leave the dwelling. Perhaps the signal was a tug on the rope or an agreed-upon message hollered from the alcove. With rope secured to the saddle horn, the brothers slowly, carefully led the animal away from the precipice, raising a swinging Clayt from canyon depths. Such daring earned Clayt the nickname "Human Plumb Bob." Gustaf Nordenskiöld noted Clayton's skill with a rope at Spring House on Wetherill Mesa.

Clayton Wetherill succeeded by a skillful cast in fastening his lasso. He then clambered up the slender rope to the ledge.

Bob Getz, Clayton's great-grandson, made a special trip to Mesa Verde

136 THE HUMAN PLUMB BOB

in 2002, retracing the steps of his great-grandfather while helping with sig-nature documentation research in a small site south of Cliff Palace called Swallow's Nest. Bob did not wait for the ladder but scrambled down the crack, lizard-like and oblivious to the need for an extension ladder. Some genes die hard!

T. Mitchell Prudden wrote of Clayt's prowess following hand- and toe-hold trails carved into the rock by the original builders.

> Clayton climbed up and found a bowl and a few potteries...
> Clayton climbed up a ledge along the line of the old foot holes in the rock and explored the ruin.

Clayton was what is termed in the business world a "floater," a person who was placed wherever the greatest need arose. He was on call to each of his brothers – Richard, John, and Al – to pinch-hit in a moment of need. As a result, he was nomadic in those early years, wandering from one loca-tion to another with his home base at the Alamo Ranch. In his adult life he would accompany many explorations with noted scientists and archae-ologists. Clayton contributed to science, as had his brothers, through qui-etly coaching his clients. He helped Al during the summer of 1893 when two Quaker women visited the Alamo Ranch. A visitor known only as E.S.K wrote a series of articles about their adventure, describing Al and Clayton only as A (Al) or C (Clayton). E.S.K. and her companion experi-enced an arduous trip filled with new adventures, taking the train from the East and coming to Mancos from the north via Vance Junction, Telluride, and Rico. Six hours after leaving Rico, the narrow gauge train reached Mancos, where they were met by a wagon from the Alamo Ranch.

The writer may have been Elizabeth S. Kite, a possible relative to the family, who along with her companion Elizabeth Snyder signed the Alamo Ranch guest register on August 11, 1893. Both women resided in Philadelphia, Pennsylvania, at the time. Whoever she was, E.S.K. pub-lished her adventures in the *Friend*, providing in vivid detail an account of what life was like at the Alamo Ranch in 1893.

> We found ourselves traveling along the wide valley of the Mancos River at this season of the year almost destitute of water, with high mountains rising up in the eastern horizon, with here and there an isolated peak to the north of us, while to the south abruptly ending spurs of the great mesa stretched out into the valley.
> The sky was clear, and the sun shone as only it can shine in this marvelous climate.
> After a ride of two miles we found ourselves confronted by a long, low, white building, shaded by tall cottonwood trees, with a beautiful asaqua flowing past. We turned and entered a large corral, enclosed

Alamo Ranch ca. 1890.

by a white fence and surrounded by numerous buildings, also white. Alighting we were led across the lawn, in which were flowers and fruit trees, and running water, to a long, low veranda, on to which seemingly innumerable rooms opened. We were there met by the sweetest of motherly souls, and felt at home at once.

This family, originally from Chester County, Pa., consists of father, mother, and five sons, the latter universally called the "boys." By dint of unceasing industry and excellent management, they have made for themselves a very oasis in a desert land. There is an air of refinement, culture and comfort over the whole place that surprises one who has heard so many stories of the "wild and woolly West."

Besides the family already described, there were a numerous train of visitors and dependants that they had aggregated. Several who had come to visit the cliffs had returned the next year to spend the whole summer in so enchanting a spot.

About twenty-five gathered daily around the tables in the dining room and kitchen while we were there. The garden supplies them with excellent vegetables and small fruits, while it only requires to go out and shoot a cow to have the larder replenished with fresh meat. They have their own irrigating reservoir, and in the winter, after the fall rains in the mountains have filled it with pure water, they collect sufficient ice to last all summer for drinking and cooking purposes, and for the laundry as well. At other seasons the water is too alkaline to be of any use in these ways.

In one of the numerous buildings surrounding the corral, is a very interesting museum, containing specimens taken from the ruins about, as well as Indian work and stuffed animals, shot on the ranch and stuffed by "the boys." But the corral itself afforded us by far the most exciting amusement. Here we had Buffalo Bill shows every night. A broncho would be lassoed and brought up to be saddled and ridden. Did you ever see a horse buck? Well, it is an interesting sight, to say the least. The animal springs into the air and bringing all four feet together, endeavors by various spasmodic actions to get through the saddle. How any one can stay on under such circumstances is hard to tell. We also amused ourselves attempting to use the lasso, never getting beyond "still life," however. A post or sometimes one of "the boys" stood for us, and my friend and I would see who could catch him first.

With Al in the lead, Clayton followed the string of visitors with a pack mule as they left for the cliff dwellings on a hot dry day. Guides in front and back worked to keep cattle and dudes moving. The mounted guide in the rear made sure no one was lost, misplaced or injured while en route. They dodged tree limbs in a dense growth of pinyon and juniper. Some time was spent in excavation, seemingly on an already heavily disturbed site, procuring a bone awl, and some human bone. Clayton would move camp ahead while visitors toured the cliff dwelling, thereby allowing for a camp to be established and dinner prepared to await the arrival of the bottom- and foot-worn guests. Clayton could not resist a bit of teasing for Elizabeth Kite. She saw him as "droll," telling her how frightened he was to have been alone in the camp before their arrival. Clayton told her of eyes watching him from the trees. The "boy" undoubtedly enhanced the women's experience by telling of "lions, tigers, and bears." Clayton would join by saying not to awaken him as he would be frightened. Their techniques would not be foreign to present-day guides when encountering unsuspecting victims unfamiliar with the wilds.

Clayton Wetherill was a major contributor to the gathering of artifacts from 1889 through 1891 when the brothers completed their largest family collection. Al Wetherill noted that Clayton and Charlie Mason made an important discovery during the winter of 1889, while much of the McLoyd and Wetherill prehistoric material from Mesa Verde was on exhibit. Excavating in the ruins of the Mesa Verde, they uncovered the mummified remains of a child in a cradle board (memorialized by Al in a poem quoted in his chapter).

Clayton was excavating in the ruins of Johnson Canyon during the winter of 1890. Deep in a canyon recess located in what is now the Ute Mountain Ute Tribal Park, he left two messages to record his working and living conditions while excavating within the cliff dwelling site. Inscriptions on pot sherds along with a broken shovel, both found years later by archaeologist Paul Nickens explained his dilemma.

Beastly cold trying to snow
1st 10th Clayton
Broke my shovel Jan. 10 1890 CW

Little is known of Clayton's role with Nordenskiöld, but at best it seems he replaced John as the packer. Clayton wrote his thoughts about Ancestral Puebloan people in an article for the *Mancos Times* in 1893. At the time he was serving as newsroom apprentice for editor W.H. "Muldoon" Kelly. Clayton discussed his vision of the Mesa Verdean people while chastising those who made outlandish assumptions. Kelly provided a flowery opening to his readership for Clayton.

To Mr. C. Wetherill of the Alamo Ranch we are indebted for the following interesting account of what has so far been ascertained regarding the Cliff dwellers in the Rio Mancos canon:

Mesa Verde National Park

Then followed Clayton's eloquent introduction on the topic.

To enter upon a subject which everyone in this section should be familiar with seems absurd, but when we hear the ruins of either the cliff houses or so-called mounds spoken of as the work of Aztec or Moqui, the question arises: What grounds has anyone for doing so, or in what respect does one compare with the other. Of course there are points of resemblance, but there are fully as many differences. The same could be said if you compare the white races with any of the neighboring Indians.

Clayton's detailed essay continued, providing an analysis including Wetherill family observations on different types of artificial skull flattening.

Clayton went on to describe differences in kivas, subterranean chambers often referred to in that era as "estufas." The round ceremonial and living structures are found associated with archaeological sites throughout

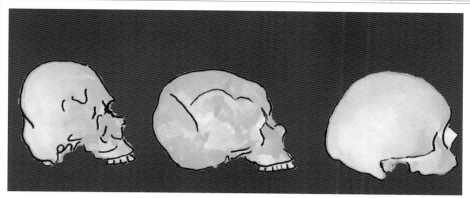

Diagram of skulls from left: Valley Dweller, Round Head and Cliff Dweller.

WETHERILLS' SKULL OBSERVATIONS

Charles McLoyd as well as the Wetherill brothers noted a difference in skull deformation among those they were uncovering. They named them the Valley Dwellers, the Cliff Dwellers, and the Round Heads. Valley Dwellers were those people found in rubble mound sites within the Montezuma Valley, such as those Ancestral Puebloans Richard identified at Snider's Well. Their skulls had been flattened by cradleboards at an oblique angle, while those of the Cliff Dweller were flattened at 90 degrees. The Round Heads represented the unde-formed skull of the Basketmakers. The Wetherills' observations may provide future researchers clues to subtle cultural difference in the "groups" of Ancestral Puebloan people.

the Four Corners. Clayton explained the spirituality of the *"Si Pa Pu,"* an emergence hole consistently found in the floors of kivas. He referred readers to the world view of archaeology in the Southwest, as presented in *Prehistoric America,* by the Marquis de Nadaillac. Frederick Chapin gave the 1884 pub-lication to Richard Wetherill as a Christmas gift in 1890. Nadaillac referred to the writings of Adolph Bandelier, James Simpson, John Wesley Powell, Lewis Henry Morgan, and William H. Holmes in one of the first attempts to understand the Cliff Dwellers of the Mesa Verde. He described these peo-ple as the Cliff Dwellers, suggesting the name was long in use by explorers prior to the Wetherill family. Clayton broadened his comparisons, most like-ly after reading Nadaillac's treatment, to include Palenque, Mexico, and the Vucay Valley in Peru. He described Wetherill family excavations in the mounds where it was typical to find bone implements on top of the ground and skeletons but a few inches below the surface.

Clayton with pack string.

Clayton continued:

> It is not the desire to detract from the interest these ancient monuments and works inspire but rather to add to it by doing away with misrepresentation and nonsensical trash and regardless of what anyone may say there always will be something that appeals to the inner most soul compelling one to respect the tombs of the ancient dead of whom we know so little.

Clayton's approach to antiquity revealed a scholarly mindset, providing cross-cultural comparisons and apparent links between existing Pueblo people and their Ancestral Puebloan forebears. His essay also expressed the sensitivity and purpose of Quaker beliefs regarding their fellow man.

Clayt was an excellent horseman known for his skills in handling and breaking broncos at the Alamo Ranch, but in 1894 he barely avoided serious injury when a horse kicked him full-on in the chest. Of all people to be kicked in the chest, this was the man whose heart had been weakened by illness six years earlier. After the accident, Clayton attended school in the Quaker community of Iowa Falls, Iowa, in 1894 and 1895, when he was in his mid-20s.

Richard and Marietta Wetherill's move to Chaco Canyon in 1897 was not completed without ready assistance from both John and Clayton. Pueblo Bonito – a large five-story Ancestral Puebloan great house in what is now Chaco Culture National Historic Park – provided Richard a setting

At left: John Wetherill and Clayton Wetherill.

Below: Business card of John and Clayton Wetherill.

John and Clayton Wetherill

TOURISTS' GUIDES
AND OUTFITTERS

TO ALL POINTS OF INTEREST
IN THE SOUTHWEST
TWENTY YEARS EXPERIENCE

PUTNAM
MCKINLEY COUNTY

NEW MEXICO

BLM Anasazi Heritage Center

for long-term massive excavation. Clayton went along as cook, with other duties as assigned.

John and Clayton teamed together during the Chaco years, creating a business card with both their names and a photograph of the two of them in full western regalia advertising their prowess as southwestern guides. Clayton accompanied Richard on the second expedition to Grand Gulch in 1897. This time he aided in the excavation while others were responsible for the livestock. John and Clayton trailed livestock owned by Richard and local Navajo families in Chaco Canyon during the drought of 1903 and 1904. Navajo and Wetherill sheep and cattle were starving so Clayton, Richard, and others drove the animals north to Aztec, New Mexico, then on to the Florida and Pine rivers, eventually reaching the headwaters of the Rio Grande via Weminuche Pass. Their efforts saved what otherwise would have been starving animals.

Perhaps Clayton Wetherill's most long lasting contributions were in T. Mitchell Prudden's expeditions. Al and Clayton often teamed together, but on one such expedition Clayton aided Prudden with an excavation that would lead to permanent nomenclature in southwestern archaeology.

Clayton with mules.

The two men excavated at Mitchell Springs in the Montezuma Valley south of the site of present-day Cortez. Mitchell Springs was the original town site for Cortez, where a large spring provided potable and palatable water for a broad area of settlement. One of the largest surviving Ancestral Puebloan surface dwellings in Montezuma County is located near the spring, and it was there that Clayton and Prudden excavated for several days. In the process, they identified a typical Pueblo II housing unit consisting of a kiva in the center of a horseshoe-shaped group of room blocks. Prudden recognized similar architectural designs in other locations. His description of those room blocks led to the modern archaeological term "Prudden Unit."

In 1914, John Wetherill called Clayton to Kayenta in what would be one of Clayton's last trips of exploration. John asked his younger brother to accompany Alfred Vincent Kidder, Samuel Guernsey, and others, from Harvard University, in their effort to excavate Basketmaker sites. Marsh Pass in northeastern Arizona was the focus of Peabody Museum excavations during the seasons of 1914-1917. Clayton and John's observation regarding similarities to Wetherill Basketmaker excavations in Grand Gulch aided Kidder and Guernsey in understanding similarities to what Richard and the Hyde brothers had deemed Basket Maker a quarter of a century before. As other researchers had been before, the Harvard scientists were impressed by Clayton's ability to gain access to archaeological sites.

Clayton Wetherill. Notice the autograph.

Clayton Wetherill and Clayton Perkins ca. 1900.

We made our entry by lashing two poles together, raising them to the edge of the cave, and steadying them with ropes while Clayton Wetherill climbed in and fastened hand-ropes. It required much daring and great skill in handling himself for this first adventurer to work from the end of the top pole, which barely reached the lip of the rock, up over the steep incline to the safe footing of the cave proper. We were without question the first people to enter this cave since its final desertion by the occupants.

Clayt developed a close friendship with Durango insurance salesman Clayton Perkins. Together they worked with Prudden as well as guiding their own individualized trips throughout the vast Southwest. Between 1909 and 1911 Perkins and Clayt guided three trips into the far reaches of the Four Corners. Their route in 1909 went to Chaco Canyon, Two Grey Hills, Black Lake, Canyon De Chelly, Del Muerto, SuraLee, Chinlee, Captain Tom Wash, and Gallego Canyon, often taking representatives of the recently formed U.S. Forest Service on tour.

Clayton wandered between his brothers' homes, helping where needed, then finally moved his family to a log cabin near Creede in 1907. Eugenia

Eugenia, baby Gilbert and Clayton in Creede.

and Clayton set up their household on Grouse Creek, seven miles from brother-in-law Charlie Mason's fisheries operation at Hermit Lakes.

Clayton was 53 when he died of heart failure in 1921 at his home near the headwaters of the Rio Grande. Prudden, upset by the loss, provided a stirring epitaph of the life of Clayton Wetherill. Several years earlier, in 1910, he had also expressed his respect for the Wetherill family while leading an inquiry into the Indian Service's role in the defamation of Richard Wetherill after his murder. Prudden's attachment to the family was heartfelt. Eugenia received T. Mitchell's tribute shortly after Clayton's death.

> I can only suggest by this word of sympathy my recognition of your great loss. My experience and enjoyment of the Southwest through many summers were so largely bound up with Clayton's helpful and genial comradeship, that I shall hardly think of it again as the same land, always beckoning one to come back.
>
> Clayton's intimate knowledge of all that great country, from the Rio Grande to the Colorado and beyond, and especially of its aborigines, was so vivid, and his experience among the ruins so great, that his passing is a serious loss to American Archaeology, which

The last photograph of Clayton Wetherill, center, before his death, standing on a cabin porch at Grouse Creek.

he and his brothers, first and last, have done so much in a quiet unostentatious way to foster.

But those of us who knew him best as a masterful leader, full of resource in all the ups and downs of these great desert spaces; ready for an emergency, knowing the secrets of the land even better than the Indians themselves, and always the cheerful and helpful comrade, we shall miss him more as a friend than as the unassuming worker for the science whose ways and aims had come to know so well. His acquaintances all over the vast country which he ranged was prodigious. Ranchers, prospectors, traders, Mexican, Indians – Navajo, Ute, Pueblo – knew Clayton and responded always, with pleased smiles and welcome to his cheery greeting. His horsemanship was superb, his knowledge of the country and its trails and water places wonderful, his energy unfailing, his endurance seemed at times without limit. All this you know better than any other, and I only write it down to mark my love and appreciation of so genial and helpful a comrade of the open road on so many strenuous journeys in the service of science.

Clayton was the second of the Wetherill brothers to die. His weakened heart stopped, succumbing to the earlier ravages of rheumatic fever. Eugenia, widowed at the age of 36 with three young children – Gilbert, Carroll, and Hilda – remained in the area and survived her husband by 43 years, dying in 1964.

WINSLOW WETHERILL

THE BLACK
SHEEP

BLM Anasazi Heritage Center

All five brothers, from left, Winslow, Al, John, Clayton and Richard.

inslow was born on July 31, 1870, in Leavenworth, Kansas, the last child of B.K. and Marian Wetherill. He proved to be the most selfish member of the Wetherill family, and he played only a small role in guiding any archaeological excavations or preservation.

Winslow resided at the Alamo Ranch when the Palmer bandwagon arrived in September 1895. Marietta (who would go on to marry Richard), was near Winslow's age and captured his interest. To impress Marietta, the young Win guided members of the Palmer family to see the cliff dwellings, but was quickly stopped by his older brother when Richard returned from the Hopi Villages. The confrontation likely created a major rift between the two.

Family oral history suggests that Winslow was sent to Iowa in 1896, for further schooling and to cool down the rivalry between the two brothers. There he met and married Mattie Pauline Young, who was five years his junior. Although family records are inconsistent on when they married, it likely was in December 1896. Many descendants think the marriage was motivated by spite or anger at Richard's plans to wed Marietta that month.

Winslow is described by his family as abusive in his marriage to Pauline, but the couple had two children: Milton, born in Cortez in 1898, and Helen, born in Iowa in 1900. Following in the footsteps of his mentoring

BLM Anasazi Heritage Center

**Pauline Young and Winslow Wetherill
in their wedding photograph.**

uncles, Milton enjoyed a long and distinguished career at the Museum of Northern Arizona. Milt's Barn on the research campus at the Museum of Northern Arizona is named after him. Helen lived with her dad during his tenure in Farmington, New Mexico. Al noted that as a young woman she could turn "ears blue" by the language she learned from her father's business associates.

Little is known about Win Wetherill's activities while at the Alamo Ranch. He was away at school when most of the big archaeological discoveries were made. Winslow was 18 at the time of the discovery of Cliff Palace in 1888. There are two known locations within Johnson Canyon in the Ute Mountain Ute Tribal Park that bear the initials WW: Turkey Track Ruin and the site where Clayton broke his shovel during the winter of 1890 while excavating for the family's major exhibit collection. So it may be assumed that Winslow briefly accompanied the expedition.

Winslow attended school in Denver before the family sent him to Oskaloosa, Iowa. By 1898, he and Pauline resided in Denver, and the following year they moved to McElmo Canyon near Cortez. In 1899, he and Pauline visited the Alamo Ranch with one-year-old Milton. Winslow's claim to fame – or infamy – was his ownership of Two Grey Hills Trading Post, which he purchased in 1902. He had worked in trading posts owned by the Hyde Exploring Expedition, undoubtedly with the help of his brother Richard. Winslow commissioned the first Navajo *Yei Bi Chai* blanket by a Navajo weaver while he owned the Two Grey Hills store. Frank McNitt, in *Richard Wetherill: Anasazi* explained what happened.

> ...Behind all of this [a conflict over supposed stolen property by a man named Harrison Hill in Mancos] was a quiet little story of a birthday gift and a trade. It seems that Win Wetherill, then the proprietor of the Two Gray [*sic*] Hills trading post, had secured

from a Navajo medicine man what may have been the first Yei-bi-chai blanket ever woven — this a reproduction of a sacred Navajo sand painting incorporating in its design, contrary to all tribal rules, the figures of Navajo Yei, or gods. The blanket came from the loom of the medicine man's wife and in its detail and workmanship, from various accounts, it was superb. At that time the making of this blanket was regarded by the Navajo as a serious break of unwritten tribal law. It has been said, although the actual circumstances are unclear, that the woman who made it and her husband who sold it to Win Wetherill were ostracized by every Navajo in the region.

Winslow Wetherill, date unknown.

Hosteen Clah, a well-known and often quoted Navajo medicine man, is believed to be the culprit, although there is some disagreement about who actually did the weaving. The resultant controversy may have contributed to Winslow selling the trading post in 1904. Win removed the *Yei Bi Chai* rug from display according to Richard Wetherill's wife Marietta, and presented it to her as a birthday gift.

Clayton and Winslow took a group of horses to Nevada in 1905. Shortly after their return, and having divorced Pauline, Winslow eloped with Eugenia Wetherill's sister Hilda and moved to Oregon. Sometime after 1910 Winslow and Hilda returned to Black Mountain Trading Post, likely running the post for the Hubbell family. At the same time, Al and Mary were residing at Salana Springs Trading Post nearby. Al and Mary's daughter Martha spent many hours together with Hilda while Winslow was on extended business trips away from the post. Hilda's memories of Black Mountain were keen and her time there one of the highlights of her life. Her classic book *Desert Wife* written in 1928 under her maiden name Hilda Faunce reflects that time, although she disguises the character names in the text.

Winslow and Richard were known as the family marksmen. In 1902 Winslow participated in a sportsman's show in Chicago, winning first prize for fancy rifle shooting. He scored 497 out of a possible 500 shots taken at a 10-cent-size bull's-eye. The trophy consisted of a large silver chalice with ivory handles. Both the rifle and trophy are now in the Wetherill Family Archives at the Anasazi Heritage Center.

At some point, Win purchased property in Farmington, New Mexico – likely while he and Hilda were operating the Black Mountain Trading Post – and Farmington became his and daughter Helen's permanent residence. After his marriage to Hilda ended, Win turned to other activities, including raising grapes and turkeys on an island in the San Juan River. Hilda moved to California, where she worked as a teacher at the California School for the Deaf. Hilda kept in touch with the Wetherill family, especially her niece Martha Wetherill Stewart. Win and Hilda had no children.

Al Wetherill suffered a most traumatic experience at Winslow's hand after Al and Mary moved from the Alamo Ranch. First Richard and then Winslow convinced him to turn over his Thoreau Trading Post inventory consisting of Navajo rugs and jewelry to be sold at the St. Louis World's Fair in 1904. Al was managing Winslow's store in Denver for the Hyde Exploring Expedition while Richard and Winslow escorted Navajo weavers and their wares to the fair. Although they sold a collection of artifacts to the Berlin Museum, and a shipment of pottery to the Chicago Field Museum, the money never materialized for Al. In fact, the entire St. Louis World's Fair was a financial disaster. The attempt to mimic the World's Columbian Exposition ended in bankruptcy. Whatever the circumstances, Al and Mary were never repaid, forcing him to abandon the Thoreau Trading Post for an appointment as the Gallup, New Mexico, postmaster.

After leaving the post office 16 years later, Al worked for Win a short time during the 1930s depression. He and Mary were treated much as indentured servants, nearly bringing Al and Win to blows but for the diplomacy of their brother John. Winslow chose a lifestyle quite different from his brothers'. His life decisions left much to be desired, yet despite it all they remained a family.

Photograph of Win taken in St. Louis 1904.

So, Who Discovered
Cliff Palace?

Cliff Palace ca. 1889. Note holes made by "besiegers."

> If you have an idea that the Weatherills [*sic*] were the first ones
> to discover the ruins at Mesa Verde, don't believe the myth.
> — Jesse Nusbaum

T he discovery of Cliff Palace is a vision – and a question – that
captures our imagination. The thought of someone stumbling
upon such a wonder conjures romantic notions of the extraordinary amidst the unknown. Many other dwellings exist within the Mesa
Verde, and likely were seen before any non-Native American saw Cliff
Palace. With its size and grandeur, though, Cliff Palace demands a discovery story. So who? How? And when?

This book is not meant to provide the Wetherills credit for discovery of
Cliff Palace, but rather to place their role within the range of early
Southwest history. Which European-American saw it first is of interest, but
only through a Eurocentric cultural viewpoint.

My research documenting historic inscriptions may help settle the con-

An 1891 Gustaf Nordenskiöld photograph of John Wetherill in Kiva D of Cliff Palace. Notice the visible inscriptions here.

troversy. Unfortunately, at least two instances of defacement and removal of the historic inscriptions within Cliff Palace prevent a final, definitive conclusion as to who was there first. I have often seen the faint traces of inscriptions, and attributed blame for removal of now historic graffiti to the National Park Service. It wasn't an unreasonable course of action for management in 1920 when Nusbaum took over as superintendent, but rather similar to the way we attempt to remove urban graffiti today. Destruction of the inscriptions/graffiti, however, lessens our chances for providing answers to the discovery puzzle. Thanks to turn-of-the-century photographs of walls and cliffs, we were able to study images that are now obscured or gone.

Within Cliff Palace we found two suspicious anomalies that suggest visits to the site before Richard and Charlie made their sighting. One is the date "1885" – three years before the Mason/Wetherill discovery – incised into the plastered wall of an inner room. The second is an undecipherable script on the wall of Kiva D, visible in a glass plate image by Gustaf Nordenskiöld. The names in plaster have long since been nearly obliterated, letters so tantalizingly close to being recognizable. Could the markings have been left by Al Wetherill as documentation sometime after his 1885 sighting? Some of the letters resemble his writing, suggesting as much.

I also researched the inscriptions found in Kiva D, one of the best preserved kivas within Cliff Palace. Hidden from public view, Kiva D's attrac-

BLM Anasazi Heritage Center

**Fred Hyde and Frederick Ward Putnam in Kiva D, 1899.
Inscriptions seen earlier are gone.**

tive plastered walls were turned into an inscription wall by the earliest visitors to Cliff Palace. Just as visitors marked their stay at the Alamo Ranch by signing the guest register, they also inscribed their names, initials and/or the date of their visit to let it be known they had been in Cliff Palace. In a Nordenskiöld photograph, John Wetherill is seen sitting on the banquette of the kiva wall. Surrounding him are many historic signatures written in charcoal or incised into the plaster. In an 1899 photograph with Frederick Ward Putnam and Fred Hyde, the majority of inscriptions on the wall are not visible. So we know someone erased or obliterated them between 1891 and 1899.

Destruction of the inscriptions therefore occurred at least seven years before Mesa Verde became a national park. Who was responsible, or why, remains a mystery. The National Park Service under the guidance of Superintendent Jesse Nusbaum continued a policy of removing inscriptions, especially in areas visible to the public. Between 1906 and 1920 when Jesse Nusbaum arrived, Mesa Verde National Park was a free-for-all, with scores of explorers, rangers, and collectors climbing into and plundering many sites. Hundreds signed their names within dwellings and on the cliff walls, making the job of identifying earlier signatures even more difficult. Artifacts were excavated illegally by appointed park rangers and sold at the ranger cabins. Jesse Fewkes expressed concern while excavating Cliff Palace in 1909, noting that upon his departure excavations and removal of artifacts were rampant. In 1919 a notice was posted to visitors in the ruins – I quote from a tattered copy with words missing:

Notice to Visitors

One may find names and dates carved into Ruins, wich [*sic*] is prohibited by the regulations of this National Park. Names may be carved upon rocks displayed, but on any rock used [by the] prehistoric inhabitants of this Mesa [it is] not only destroying the authen[tic] [unreadable] such Rock, but it is absolutely forbidden and punishable by law.

Nusbaum was a staunch critic of the belief that the Wetherills were the first to "discover" Cliff Palace. He worked hard from 1930 into the 1970s in an attempt to pin down an exact accounting of that discovery, conducting numerous oral history interviews of those who had the opportunity to view the cliff dwelling early on. Nusbaum's tenacious research combines here with my inscription documentation to weave the stories of those early viewings of Mesa Verde's cliff dwellings. Many had the opportunity before the Wetherills, as Nusbaum observed.

Mesa Verde National Park

Jesse Nusbaum

Was Cliff Palace discovered when someone saw it from a distance? Hadn't it already been discovered in this way by untold numbers of Utes in the centuries since the Ancestral Puebloans left? Or was it discovered only when someone climbed into Cliff Palace and examined it close-up? If that is the case, isn't it still possible that Utes discovered Cliff Palace long before any EuroAmericans came on the scene? Perhaps, though, the only discovery that counts is the one that triggered widespread public interest.

The most obvious answer as to who "discovered" Cliff Palace is the Utes. They understood canyons and mesas. They were familiar with what stood among them, yet culturally respectful, thereby choosing not to enter the abandoned dwellings. Their term for these ancient

Fred Blackburn Collection/Courtesy of John Richardson

Sandal House, formerly known as First Ruin. This photo was taken by H. Jay Smith in 1892.

people is *Moquitch*. The fact that Acowitz, a Ute, talked about the cliff dwellings and may have shown them to the Wetherills is an excellent demonstration of their prior knowledge. That prior claim prompts an interesting question regarding management of those sites. Given their attitude and respect for the dwellings, wouldn't they have been better preserved if the Utes had prohibited entry into them?

Sandal House within the Ute Mountain Ute Tribal Park is the "Rosetta Stone" inscription site for all of Mancos Canyon. First Ruin, as it was originally known, was a prominent landmark for those who traveled through the Mancos Canyon, and the inscriptions left there had escaped destruction until recent time. Many questions and answers about those travelers and explorers are found here, providing this historian with a detailed glimpse into the past. Fortunately, we were able to document the inscriptions before a back wall collapsed, obliterating much of the historic graffiti.

Inscriptions, which are found in most major cliff dwellings, provide clues to who may have visited them first. In turn, those clues may help us solve the puzzle of who viewed Cliff Palace first.

Juan Antonio Maria Rivera 1765, Dominguez and Escalante 1776

Spanish arrival into the Four Corners presented the first opportunities for non-natives to see the cliff dwellings. But explorers Juan Antonio Maria Rivera in 1765 and Dominguez and Escalante in 1776 missed that opportunity because of their guide. An unamed ex-slave and a man of "mixed blood" including Ute, he intentionally diverted both parties, first Rivera and then Dominguez and Escalante away from the Mesa Verde. Instead, he turned them north toward the Dolores River where they would establish the earliest European record (1776) of the prehistoric dwellings on a knoll near the present-day Anasazi Heritage Center. The guide made a substantial effort to discourage the parties from traveling into the canyons of the Mancos River. Perhaps he feared being recaptured, or more likely he shared the Ute belief that the *Moquitch* should not be disturbed.

T. Stangl 1861

The first and most likely opportunity for viewing Cliff Palace is suggested by the inscription of "T. Stangl" carved deeply and carefully into the stone wall at the eastern edge of Bone Awl House. The cliff dwelling is located in a small side canyon southeast of Balcony House, within the Ute Mountain Ute Tribal Park. Without documents naming Stangl or explaining his presence in the region, it is difficult to know what brought him to Bone Awl House. But several exploration parties and individual prospectors were scouring the mountains in search of gold at that time. Charles Baker led a group into the Animas River drainage above present-day Silverton, established a town site and found small amounts of placer gold. His exaggerated claims inspired hundreds of men to join them in Baker's Park. Stangl may have been one of them.

But he also might have been part of a group led by Doc Arnold that took a wrong turn on the way to Baker's Park and ended up in the Uncompahgre Valley near present-day Ouray in the winter of 1860-61. In either case, the men who sought gold in the San Juan Mountains encountered harsh winter conditions. Remains of Engelmann spruce cut for firewood 20 to 30 feet above the ground in Starvation Gulch in the Rio Grande drainage east of Baker's Park provide stark reminders of how deep the snow lay upon the camps of speculators and prospectors through the winter of 1860. Arnold's group fared somewhat better than the prospectors in Baker's Park, thanks to hot springs and a good supply of provisions.

Harsh conditions combined with the scarcity of placer gold were enough to persuade some prospectors to give up on the area and move on. Development of the area died within two years from lack of gold and onset of the Civil War. In the spring of 1861, faced with deep snows in the mountains to the south of them, Arnold's party followed the Spanish Trail south along the San Miguel, Dolores and Mancos rivers, eventually circling

John Moss and Ernest Ingersoll at Two Story Ruin in Mancos Canyon ca. 1874.

back east and north to the first Animas City, about 20 miles north of present-day Durango. It is possible that they explored the Mancos Canyon in the course of that journey.

Nusbaum remained perplexed regarding how Stangl came to be in the Mesa Verde. He speculated that he may have been from a "small independent trading party," or a "maverick group of Mormons from Utah."

Wherever he had been, Stangl entered Bone Awl House in 1861 and signed his name and date. The likelihood of his finding Cliff Palace, though, is slim. Cliff Canyon is rugged, and Stangl was probably weakened by his journey, both factors that would have dissuaded him from choosing such a difficult path. Nonetheless, he and perhaps his party would have been the first documented European Americans to view at least some of the cliff dwellings of the Mesa Verde.

John Moss and Harry Lee 1872, 1873

Eleven years after Stangl carved his name in Bone Awl House, Captain John Moss came to the Mesa Verde in search of silver. Moss had recently completed his mining ventures in the Mojave Desert while convincing the Parrott brothers, San Francisco bankers, there was wealth to be found in the La Plata Mountains. He, or perhaps his scouts, headed east in 1872,

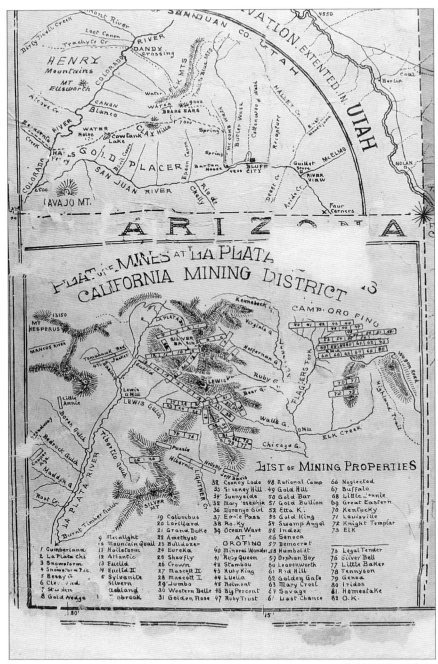

John Moss's California Mining District 1893.

crossing the Colorado River at Lee's Ferry. Moss and a Ute-speaking friend named Harry Lee passed through the "Monumental Valley," then followed the De Chelle River to the San Juan, and on to the Mancos River. Moss formed the California Mining District, dividing the canyons and peaks of the La Plata Mountains into individual claims. His activities resulted in the first settlement to grow out of the quest for silver along the banks of the La Plata River. By 1873, prospectors were looking for silver everywhere in the San Juans.

The Parrott brothers were bankers in Mexico prior to their arrival in San Francisco, and so may have been privy to information regarding Spanish discovery and mining of silver in the La Plata Mountains prior to 1823. They may have discussed what they knew about the location with Moss in terms of a speculative mining venture. Gathering such information was something Moss excelled in, as he seldom if ever put a pick in the ground. He relied instead on hard-working prospectors spilling their information over a glass of whisky. Moss honored his sponsors by naming the first settlement – located where La Plata Canyon emerges from the mountains – Parrott City. Moss accompanied or sent an advance party to search the route to Parrott City in 1872. A year later in 1873 Moss and Harry Lee led a group of settlers to the chosen settlement location.

Evidence of their passing through is found in the form of initials and a date of 1872 on the prehistoric masonry of Sandal House. Legends persist that Moss took the first photographs of cliff dwellings, but no surviving photographs are attributed to him. The tale likely refers to his guiding William Henry Jackson and Ernest Ingersoll of the Hayden Survey Party in 1874. Moss, and his men, may very well have been the second group of EuroAmericans to view cliff dwellings along the Mancos River. Moss brought a settlement group with him in 1873. Their destination was the designated location for Parrot City. There was little time for perusing the side canyons of the Mesa Verde or exploring hidden dwellings such as Cliff Palace when their focus was on pioneering a permanent settlement.

Hayden Survey Party 1874, 1875

W.H. Holmes wrote in his 1875 journal that Jackson, Ingersoll, and Moss penciled their inscriptions within Two Story Ruin in the present-day Ute Mountain Ute Tribal Park. I believe I found the location there, on an eastern plastered wall. All but the traces of lead and lines for three names have been obliterated. The people who left their inscriptions did not usually write with large, ornate letters, at least in the early years of exploration. As if in awe of their discovery, they tried to be unobtrusive when recording their presence.

Two Story Ruin is the first cliff dwelling photographed by William Henry Jackson. From there, the Hayden Survey party continued west and south down Mancos Canyon before turning north then west once again where McElmo Canyon provided a route of travel. A year later William H. Holmes returned to the canyon, this time from the west, and excavated

Sixteen Window House, the first recorded excavation within Mancos Canyon. There are no surviving inscriptions from the Hayden Surveys of 1874 or 1875 in the canyons sheltering Cliff Palace and Balcony House. They kept on the straight and narrow route along the Mancos River.

Chapman Ballard 1875

After news spread of Moss's visit and Jackson's photographs, Mancos Canyon was overrun with explorers in the late 1870s and early 1880s. Inscription evidence consistently indicates these groups and individuals stayed in the canyon bottom, often turning back after reaching Sandal House. There is at least one exception, Chapman Ballard. Nusbaum in about 1940, recounted Ballard's discomfort when hearing the Wetherills were being credited with discovering Cliff Palace.

> He [Francis Cheetham, local attorney and historian of Santa Fe] said that Chapman Ballard, cherished friend and long time local rancher was mad as hell about this Wetherill claim of discovery, said he would refute this and write the true story about its discovery, while he was on the 1875 Survey of the North Boundary of the Southern Ute Reservation, and get on with it right away. When I next saw Cheetham, he told me Ballard had died suddenly – that he had never reviewed a single portion of such a report.

Ballard did make his claim of discovery known in a letter to the editor of the *Mancos Times Tribune* on February 14, 1936.

> I saw an article stating that Richard and Alferd [*sic*] Wetherill were the discoverer [*sic*] of the Cliff Palace in Mesa Verde National Park in the year of 1888. It may be of interest to you to know that a party of surveyors discovered it as well as other ruins in that vicinity, thirteen years before the Wetherills first saw it. The party was engaged in surveying a block of ground purchased from the Ute Indians by the government and known as the San Juan County.
>
> We first saw the Cliff Palace from about the same spot the Wetherills first saw it. We dropped everything, crossed the canon and climbed into the palace, where we spent some time looking it over. The survey was made by the contractor, Darling. The chief engineer's name was Jim Miller and a brother of the contractor, Bob Darling, was one of the party as guide and interpreter.
>
> This survey was made the Summer of 1875 and if any one might wish to verify this statement, I think they will find a record of the survey and the date thereof in the surveyor feneral's [*sic*] office, Washington D. C.
>
> Signed: Chapman Ballard, Taos, N.M.

Ballard proved to be accurate in his statements about the survey. He is listed along with other crew members S.C. Aston and H.B. Clifford, both chainmen, and E.F. Saunders, flagman. A letter from the Colorado Land Office dated February 4, 1970, confirmed that James W. Miller was issued a contract for survey on October 2, 1874, but there is no mention of cliff dwellings in Miller's final report. W. S. Wills of the General Land Office in Washington, D.C., wrote to Jesse Nusbaum about the matter on June 15, 1945.

> The field note records here show that C. Ballard served as axeman with James W. Miller, U.S. Deputy Surveyor, on the surveys of the north boundary of the Ute Indian reservation under contract dated October 2, 1874, survey executed October 2, October 23, 1875; and also on the survey of the boundaries of the Ute ceded land. These surveys were in the general vicinity of the Cliff Palace and the record shows that the surveyors detoured long distances north and south of the surveyed boundary line in order to find suitable places to cross the canyons which had precipitous sides. These voluminous field notes have been scanned but no reference to the Cliff Palace was observed...

Nusbaum in a letter dated February 12, 1970, added more to the Ballard story, as told to him by Francis Cheetham. That information lends further credibility to Ballard's claim.

> ...It was while we were running the North Line of the Southern Ute Indian reservation that we saw the Mesa Verde ruins. I think it must have been in July. I do not know what one of us first saw Cliff Palace, but it could be seen plainly from where we were working. We were on the opposite side of the canyon, but we all went to it at once, and inspected it, and other ruins, seeing much broken pottery around. The discovery created much interest among us. Whether it was mentioned in the report of the survey I don't know.

Nusbaum believed Ballard's claim, but unfortunately relatives in Oklahoma had possession of his journal and would not share it in the belief it would be worth a considerable amount of money. The trail for his discoveries ran dry without documentation. While surveying boundary lines in 1913, the National Park Service conducted a detailed search for pinyon pines with ax blazes cut as boundary marks by the Miller party in 1875. They found only a single remaining tree in Prater Canyon, east of Cliff Canyon. The marker trees closest to Cliff Palace and crucial to verify-

Animas Museum

Richard Gaines ca. 1875.

ing Chapman Ballard's claims were nowhere to be found.

Ballard's purported discovery while conducting a survey in 1875, as well as that of S.E. Osborn who was prospecting for coal in 1884 (see below), must weigh in on the side of credibility. The circumstances of their explorations placed them in rugged upper canyons and drainages.

Mancos Canyon remained the main route of travel to the west and south throughout the 1870s. Readily available water and forage for animals plus a mild winter climate made the route most appealing. Many traveled it without having any specific reason to venture into the side canyons as Ballard and Osborn had. Claims of those other individuals are more suspect.

Richard Gaines and Carlos Stebbins 1875

Richard Gaines and Carlos Stebbins, early settlers of Animas City who traveled together through Mancos Canyon, provide insight into what normal travel conditions and encounters with Utes were like there. Gaines' journal includes a brief explanation of the purpose for their trip. The two men were young entrepreneurs who sought to make a quick fortune by selling goods from Animas City to the Navajos along the San Juan River. They spent the first night of their trading trip with Hans Aspaas, an early settler along the Animas and La Plata rivers. They trapped a few mink while there, then moved on into the narrow Mancos Canyon. They noted the presence of four settlers from Moss's party who had homesteaded along the river. On December 22, 1875, Gaines wrote about what they saw that day.

> We are camped toknight Halloed ground for it twas trod by the mysterious departed of Centurys ago And they have left nothing behind to tell the tale. But pieces of crockery and ruined houses. We found one today High up on the Cliff under a shelving rock. The walls are standing yet to four rooms and two reservoirs [kivas]. On one wall is a drawing of a man and also on one wall there is a mark of a hand it looks like they had put their hand in white wash then in the wall. I do not think any other white

man ever saw this house for it was by chance that I found it.

Gaines' description fits that of Sandal House. In the midst of his excitement, Gaines may not have noticed small penciled inscriptions left by others such as Moss's party that had previously viewed and visited the ruin. Gaines recorded a peaceful meeting with several Southern Utes along the way; Mancos Jim and Red Jacket (Ignacio) of the Weminuche band were specifically mentioned. But the two men were not so fortunate when they encountered Navajos. Their trip ended in a gun battle with the Navajos and they lost all their trade goods.

Henry Morgan 1875-1890

Henry Morgan was a cattleman who grazed his stock on the upper mesas and canyons of the Mesa Verde from the early 1870s through the mid-1880s. As with Ballard and Osborn, Morgan's reasons for touring the upper drainages were different from most visitors to the canyon country.

Morgan ran Texas longhorn cattle as draft oxen in Mancos Canyon before tensions with the Utes caused many of the cattlemen to leave. At the peak of his freighting business, Morgan cared for 56 draft animals. He was particularly proud of one team of his cattle whose horns spanned nearly seven feet.

Morgan arrived in the Mancos Valley freighting a sawmill to Parrott City for Captain John Moss. When he talked with the 96-year-old former freighter, Nusbaum deemed him one of the brightest people that age he had ever interviewed. Morgan explained how his cattle and the Wetherill cattle often intermingled. Even though their ranges differed, their cattle would mix when Morgan brought his oxen off the high, side canyon ridges of the Mancos Canyon. Nusbaum described what Morgan told him.

> ... he was living in a little log house on the Mancos River below present Mancos when a little dark complexioned man rode up to his door on a little brown stallion, said he was B.K. Wetherill, that he had decided that he wanted to build a home for his family in the grove of cottonwoods across the river but he could not bring them there till the home was completed – that he was scared to death of the Utes who were rampaging about the country – would like to live with him until he could go back east for his family. Henry said he could, and would welcome him as a neighbor – that he was one of the three bachelors then living in Mancos Valley – that there were no women in those parts and his wife would also be welcomed.

Morgan also had a reason to be in remote canyon areas containing cliff dwellings. He told Nusbaum of his tracking big longhorn cattle up the north slope of the Mesa Verde canyon country through dense vegetation, no simple task in the 1870s.

> ...he tracked them up that climb on horse back, then down Bear Canyon as the prospectors called it – Ruin Canyon next, then later Soda Canyon to this time – that it was nearly impossible to get thru because of the denseness of scrub oak, shrubbery and pinon and cedar cover. Said his prize lead team of cattle got thru it some way, and he had a tough time following them back – had to stop over night at the spring – Soda Spring – both hobbled and tied his horse and kept a fire burning, as the bears were numerous and spooked his horse time and again. They were probably coming there for water. He got his cattle down to the valley floor the next day. In this context he asked me to let him know if I ever, in the course of my rambling about the Mesa Verde region, ever ran across a wooden ox yoke painted blue – that he always painted his yoke blue and wanted to relocate one.

Al Wetherill also wrote of the many bears in Mancos Canyon. He indicated that many of them were black but there were also grizzlies – which the Wetherill family called "Range Bears" – that occasionally made trips from the mesa into the canyon. Brush and bears provided excellent reasons for most travelers to avoid exploration of side canyons like the one where Cliff Palace remained hidden.

Nusbaum asked Morgan about his knowledge of ruins on Mesa Verde and place names. Morgan explained that his cattle worked down-canyon while the Wetherill cattle worked up-canyon. Morgan had the tougher job and the opportunity for earlier archaeological discoveries. Morgan's response to Nusbaum's question reflected his lack of interest toward cliff dwellings. He said that he had probably seen all of the more conspicuous cliff dwellings and ruins but had only entered a few of them – he did not know which ones because none of them had been named at the time. Morgan indicated he also knew S.E. Osborn, who explored the canyon in 1884. My belief is that Morgan was more likely referring to George W. Jones, a fellow oxen freighter with whom he was undoubtedly acquainted. Jones played a freighting role in the 1884 discoveries by Osborn and William Henry Hayes. I am not sure of Morgan's dates in the canyon but likely he was in the area from 1879 with the arrival of B.K. Wetherill until the discovery. A single inscription from a "Dick Morgan" is found in Cliff Palace, most likely placed at a later date by an unrelated individual.

Gonzales Rash and Clyde Bonnel 1876

Gonzales Rash and Clyde Bonnel were very likely early travelers in Mancos Canyon. They left their signatures while exploring Sixteen

Window House in 1876. We know nothing of the men but their signatures are part of an increase in the number of signings during the mid-1870s, in turn reflecting increased travel within Mancos Canyon.

Lewis Henry Morgan 1878

Lewis Henry Morgan (not related to Henry Morgan) considered by some as the father of the field of anthropology, arrived in Mancos Canyon in 1878. As many who would follow the steps of the Hayden Survey (which was made available to the public that year), Morgan utilized their reports to retrace the surveyors' journey.

Morgan's route was typical of the day, following the main course of the Mancos River. He kept detailed notes and illustrations of archaeological sites he found, the first scientific documentation of the archaeological record within Mancos Canyon.

Morgan developed theories of "primitive communism" while working with the Seneca and Iroquois tribes in the 1840s. In 1881 his *Houses and House Life of the American Aborigines* discussed southwestern examples of communal behavior and community life practiced by modern Pueblos. Morgan's theories served as inspiration for Karl Marx, who had written to him about his ideas as early as 1848. Although the American's views differed from Marx's final doctrine, his writings helped shape Marx's *Communist Manifesto*.

Thomas Chestnut and Charles Bayles 1878

The Hayden Survey publication of 1878 contained both archaeological and geological information concerning potential for mineral and mining development in the region. Prospectors pored over every detail of the report searching for another area of potential wealth. While reading the report, many became curious about cliff dwellings. When time allowed, which was not often, a few made extended side trips to view the cliff dwellings.

Such was the case for Thomas Chestnut and Charles Bayles of Silverton in 1878. Both men were members of the Silverton Bachelor Group. Formed in nearly womanless societies within the mining camps, such groups predated many modern fraternal organizations and provided mutual support for men who had no family with them. These men honored not cheating each other and helping one another in times of need – a male support system within the camps. They more often than not died young or were injured in the dangerous professions they chose or the adventures they pursued in their limited free time. Chestnut delivered mail in the winter between Silverton and Del Norte while Bayles was postmaster of Silverton. They arrived at Sandal House in 1878 and where they left their names. Bayles had stopped at the out-of-the-way attraction on his way home to visit family in Des Moines, Iowa – his first trip home in 10 years.

Samuel Burghardt and A.D. Morrison 1880

Two miners left their signatures in Sandal House in 1880. Samuel Burghardt, first county commissioner of Dolores County, and A.D. Morrison, a cattleman from the Dolores River, were members of the Rico chapter of the "Benevolent Order of Bachelors." They were both residing in Rico when they made a quick trip to Sandal House.

In a 1927 affidavit, Walter Morrison, very likely related to A.D. Morrison, along with an R.E. Keith, stated they discovered the cliff dwellings in 1883.

> We the undersigned, Citizens of Colorado, claim to be the original discoverers of the Mesa Verde Ruins having discovered them August 1883. They were found while hunting horses for old Spud Hudson (a big cattleman) who headquarters were at that time Blue Mountains, Utah, or who is now called Monticella [sic], Utah. We can furnish more proof of this discovery if necessary.

(J.A.) James Frink, R.B. Adams, J.E. Ptolemy, John Reid, Theodore Wattles 1881

James Frink and a group of men from the newly formed community of Mancos arrived in Mancos Canyon in 1881 with the specific purpose of exploring ruins. Frink was an early settler in the Mancos Valley, cattleman, banker, and sometime guide to the cliff dwellings. Wattles was one of the two possible people who told Al Wetherill about Balcony House and the artifacts found within it. Wattles was a prospector, born in Mercer County, Ohio, on May 25, 1840. Nothing is known about R.B. Adams. J.E. Ptolemy was born on April 15, 1857, later marrying the daughter of prominent cattleman Major Daniel Sheets. The Ptolemys arrived in Mancos in 1877 from Hamilton, Ontario, Canada.

J.E. Ptolemy's brother R.W. recorded the family's movement of cattle in the Mancos Canyon area in an article for the *Montezuma Valley Journal* in August of 1943. Early newspaper accounts acknowledged the continual presence of the "Border Ruffians," referring to the Navajo who lived north of the San Juan River. Their presence north of the river was significant enough that two springs were named after them: Navajo Springs near Towaoc, Colorado, and Little Navajo Springs farther west.

> At that time says Mr. Ptolemy, what is now the Navajo Nation was open range, now closed to the paleface cattleman, it was then open. Navajo Springs was the summer camp for all the outfits operating out of there because of the never failing fine spring of water, which Mr. Ptolemy says, is still flowing as sweet, as strong, as cold as it did in those days. This was pretty much a no mans land until after the Brunot Treaty forced the Utes into the area.

The five men placed their names and the date on a prehistoric door slab, then turned it inward to the trunk of a large juniper tree near Sixteen Window House where it lay until discovered by Kenneth Douthett during our inscription research within Ute Mountain Ute Tribal Park in 1996. Their names either individually or collectively are found in dwellings from Two Story Ruin at the mouth of Soda Canyon to Sixteen Window House farther west in main Mancos Canyon. All sites visited by the Mancos group are located within Ute Mountain Ute Tribal Park.

While excavating Cliff Palace in 1909, Jesse Fewkes used Frink as his only primary source for information about early excavation within Cliff

Fred Blackburn Collection/Courtesy of Robert Ptolemy

J.E. Ptolemy

Palace. Frink was one of three men to hold cattle leases within the established Mesa Verde National Park. He told Fewkes he was the first to discover Cliff Palace, which Fewkes noted in his 1910 report on the Cliff Palace excavation.

> ...But several residents of the towns of Mancos and Cortez claim to have visited it before that time [referring to the Mason/Wetherill discovery in December of 1888]. One of the first was a cattle owner of Mancos, Mr. James Frink, who told the author that he first saw Cliff Palace in 1881, and as several stock men were with him at the time it is probable that there were others who visited it the same year...

Troweling Through Time, by Florence Lister, contains a photo labeled "J.C. Frick," who guided Nusbaum and Kidder; it likely is J.A. Frink. The chances of Frink being the first to sight Cliff Palace are minimal, however. I found no inscriptions related to him or his party of men within Soda, Cliff, or Navajo canyons. I suspect his claimed discovery was actually Sixteen Window House in Mancos Canyon, which he later attempted to represent as Cliff Palace. Frank McNitt wrote of Frink's involvement in Cliff Palace in *Richard Wetherill: Anasazi.*

> Archaeologists who followed Fewkes to Mesa Verde were interested enough to call upon Jim Frink and press him for details.

Each time he was asked to describe Cliff Palace as he first saw it, Frink gave conflicting answers. Shortly before his death, he as much as admitted there had been no truth in what he had told Jesse Fewkes.

S.E. Osborn, William Henry Hayes, George W. Jones 1884

S.E. Osborn, William Henry Hayes, and George W. Jones arrived in Mancos Canyon in 1884. They explored the side and upper drainages of the Mancos River. Osborn signed his name on a stone slab in Hemenway 1, as being from Burlington, Iowa. The stone slab has since been stolen, although the place it once rested remains apparent.

Osborn's directive while in Mancos Canyon was to research coal seams which coincidentally were very near the levels of major cliff dwellings. His, Hayes', and Jones' signatures occur throughout Soda Canyon and at Swallows Nest, located approximately one-half mile down Cliff Canyon on the same level and canyon side as Cliff Palace. All dates are from 1884.

Kathy Fiero, long-term stabilization team leader at Mesa Verde National Park, and I concluded while working in Balcony House, that Osborn's description, written first in the *Denver Times* in 1886 and reprinted in the *Rico Times* in 1890, is actually a potpourri of experiences within cliff dwellings they visited and excavated. The majority of Osborn's description fits Balcony House, which I am certain they were the first to excavate. There is some room for doubt, however, that the entire description is from Balcony House.

Osborn's description better fits Balcony House, including its location in "Bear Canon," an early name for Soda Canyon. One lone element of his description, though, hints also of Cliff Palace.

> ...but I was well paid for my trouble finding a building at least 250 feet in length six stories in height in front and from four to six rooms deep into the cliff. This seems to have been a chief's house, or Pan-electric director, or perhaps a boodle man.

As for Osborn's speculations, a "boodle" is a collection or group of people; a "boodle man" is in charge of such a group. It's unknown just what he meant by "Pan-electric director," although it may bear some connection to Pan, the Greek god of shepherds and hunters as well as the creator of the pan pipe.

Perhaps Osborn viewed Cliff Palace and was describing Speaker Chief House within Cliff Palace. Detailed comparison pertaining to the length suggests his site description refers to Balcony House, but four rooms deep and six stories high suggests Cliff Palace. If Osborn did, in fact, view Cliff Palace he neglected to mention a very prominent tower in the western section.

His motivation for writing the 1886 article quoted here may have derived from an article of the same period published by Virginia McClurg, who asserted that she was the first person to set foot in the dust of Balcony House. Osborn knew minute details of Balcony House's artifacts and architecture from his earlier excavation, and logically would have provided essential details to

Fred Blackburn Collection/Courtesy Shirley Kennedy

Mary Ann Hammond Hayes and William Henry Hayes

the Denver and Telluride newspapers concerning the discovery of Balcony House to refute McClurg's claim of discovery. There was no need, in that context, for Osborn to describe Cliff Palace in detail, so he offered only a single descriptive hint of having been there.

On another note, though, Osborn stated they left artifacts in place. That may be untrue as he and his men were responsible for removal of dwelling contents they found in Soda and Cliff canyons.

> During my stay in the canyon I gathered dozens, yes hundreds of relics that would have made the heart of an antiquarian glad, but did not carry any away with me when I left.

I consider it extremely likely that Osborn, Hayes and/or Jones at the very least *viewed* Cliff Palace. Not all men signed in every ruin they entered, suggesting perhaps that each had established a territory for excavation or was assigned to those specific dwellings. Due to the erasure and destruction of names within Cliff Palace, there is little chance of ever fully answering the question of whether they visited there.

Henry Goodman 1885

Henry Goodman homesteaded his cattle operation on the Utah/Colorado border. Goodman Point and Goodman Point Ruin west of Cortez are named after him. Goodman later described in an interview what he claimed occurred in 1885.

> While grazing a herd along the western base of the Mesa he found that a number of his horses were missing. He tracked them to the top of the Mesa and back along the rim of a long canyon. Looking across, he was astonished to see the wondrous Anasazi complex, now called the Cliff Palace. He had seen many ruins

before, but none quite of this magnitude. Later he heard of the Wetherill interest in ruins and told them what he had seen.

Goodman's account is remarkably similar to that described by Charlie Mason and Richard Wetherill in 1888.

Al Wetherill 1885;
Charlie Mason, Richard Wetherill, December 16, 1888

The sightings by Al Wetherill in 1885 and Richard Wetherill and Charlie Mason in 1888 are discussed in the chapters about them. Al's discovery claim is backed by a sequence of historic inscriptions following his described route in 1885. Versions represented by Marietta are often suspect due to her tendency to exaggerate when telling stories, yet in this case many of the facts match, particularly regarding Al Wetherill's map showing the route followed. The 1917 Charlie Mason article remains the most accurate and detailed account of the sighting and first visit.

Of all claims to discovery, only three before Al's viewing in 1885 and Richard and Charlie Mason's well-recorded sighting on December 16, 1888, seem credible.

Chapman Ballard (1875) and Henry Morgan (circa 1878-1879) most likely viewed Cliff Palace. Osborn, Hayes, and Jones may have excavated a small portion of the site in 1884. Yet none, other than Osborn, and perhaps Chapman in his inaccessible journal, chose to record even minimal notes or details about what they found.

As for the other claims of discovery, such latter-day "recollections" likely had as much to do with a desire for notoriety as historic accuracy. Some wished to have egos stoked as "discoverers," whether true or not.

An 1893 Visit to Cliff Palace

Access to Cliff Palace remained quite difficult for many years after the first non-Native Americans entered it. Spurred by his visit to a Chacoan Great House near Spring Creek in Montezuma County, Leander Hayes organized an expedition to Cliff Palace in November 1893. His recounting of both the journey and their activities once in the cliff dwelling lend valuable insight into the attitudes of the day.

His brother William Henry disliked the Wetherills. Wetherill fame in the rediscovery of Cliff Palace must have been galling for him, since he was well aware of the archaeological sites in Cliff and Soda canyons. This friction may have been the root not only of the accusations about the Wetherills' purported use of dynamite but also for William Henry Hayes' complaint against them and their subsequent arrest in 1892.

Leander's journal entries about their trip to Sandal House and Cliff Palace are some of the clearest observations recorded by a visitor yet found from that era.

"To the Ruins of the Ancient Cliff Dwellers"

On Wednes-morning Nov 15th 1893 We started six in company from Wm Henrys to visit some of the Most wonderful ruins in the whole world. Perhaps the oldest extant. Our Guide Mr. Hugo Weston. Will Wood & Mary. Nellie & Willie Hayes and myself....

Our wagon was loaded with bedding, cooking utensils and provission to last till our return in perhaps 2 days. Our purpose chiefly is to reach a noted ruin, here called Cliff Pallace containing 157 rooms. It is on the Ute Indian Reservation.

...Soon we are in the canon. Narrow and deep. High steep Mountains on each side, and at times comeing down to the very creek. in such places we are compelled to climb the Mountains and single file to creep along slowly on a narrow trail not over 12 inches wide. beneath us the Mancos is rushing among the boulders which nearly fill its narrow bed.

I managed to stick on with difficulty, and my knees. at last we all made it safely. Oh what a climb for a horse to make and carrie a rider too. But my wonder increased when I looked upon this wondrous ruin [Sandal House]. It was in view before I dismounted, but I was so profoundly interested and occupied in keeping on, that I hadent seen it. As I looked upon this ruin I was suprized beyond expression. So peculiarly constructed in such a peculiar place. So different from anything I had ever seen before ...

We now began to see other canons entering into Mancos Canon. Our Guide is carefully studying each one on our right for Cliff Canon. It requires great care, for to me they all look alike. Our Guide while familiar with Mancos and Other Canons had never visited Cliff Canon, but he had informed himself and was capable for the task. We had to take down brush fences the Indians had made. Guide passed the word to leave them down...

...we followed on up this canon until about 2 O Clock P.M. when we came to a gorge so immense we had to halt. we could go no farther and were compelled to take back track for water.

Our Guide was quite sure that we were near Cliff Palace. He concluded we should camp for the night here, and after supper he and Mr. Wood would try to find it. They started about 4 P.M. ...

The route their guide chose to follow was an especially difficult one, east of that favored by the Wetherills. The following morning, they continued.

Finally we came to a Mighty gorge indeed. we could not see beyond this one. Boulders large and small thousands of them, from the size of a table to that of a wood shed choked it up, how far, we couldnt tell. ... The men now had to make our trail ...

Three days after their departure from Mancos, on November 17, 1893, they reached their destination.

Our guide has gained a foothold on the upper side somehow and throws his rope to us, and thus one by one we ascend its steep smoth sides. On up, up, higher and yet higher, lean against a rock to rest, pull by another, then a good step or two, soon we come in sight of Cliff Palace. Wonder, and a feeling of awe took possession of us as we first looked upon this ancient ruins. Tis a huge affair. Here is the work of a race of People of whom we to day know nothing ...

I will now try as best I may be able to give you a pen picture of these wonderful ruins. However, they must be seen to be under- stood. Her, tis now, a lonely place. So dessolate, with the stillness of death all about it. hiden away in these Mountain fastnesses, away up the mountains side which beasts of burden can not reach ... Away up above us, over to our left, we discover a cavity directly under a great rock, as we approach we find this opening growing larger. the craggy tops of broken walls begin to be seen. These increase in number as we get higher, and nearer. Soon, It all at once burst upon our sight. A feeling of awe, and Something akin to Superstition, seems to take hold of us. Do the spirits of the departed hover near ...

Leander wrote disparagingly of earlier visitors to the ruins, condemning their artifact collecting and alleged use of explosives to gain access to inner rooms. Nonetheless, he and his party excitedly collected whatever they could find. At some point after returning to Missouri, Leander donated his artifact collection to a university there.

...but few whites have ever been here, a very few, and they are well known. have wrought sad havoc with mattock and spade and dynamite. digging for relics, opening graves for Mummies etc. I visited Wetherills whose ranch is near Mancos, and examined their collection. They had an exhibit of it at the worlds fair at Chicago in 1893 ...

I soon turned my attention to collecting relics. relics of any thing pertaining to those ancient people, and I succeeded quite well. Secureing pieces of potery, of course, broken pieces of quaint painted designs also some indented ware. Corn husks, Corn Cobs, Strings just as they made them and plainly showing the mark of the stone ax. Stone trowel, Bade Stone. I also gathered a number of their bones, principally in one room.

Mr. Weston noticed over head a string hanging from the ceiling in the mortar. It evidently for some special purpose had been built in with the mortar. Mr. Weston broke the piece off from the wall that contained the string and brought it to me. I question if it can be duplicated today in the world.

We gathered my collection of Relics together. I had a large haversack and strap to go over my shoulder. Mary had two 50 lb flour sacks carrying provision, but, now empty. we filled these. Jenny had a sack and all six of us had a fair load to carry.

Summary

We may never know for certain what sightings and events followed early discoveries of Cliff Palace. Obviously a strong opportunity existed during the mid- to late-1870s, and early in the 1880s. Perhaps somewhere in an unknown diary, a dark back room, on the stone wall of an alcove, under a blackened beam, or perhaps hidden on a stone, is a fine-lined penciled message that some future researcher will find and link to a claim of discovery. Until that moment, documentation in the form of writing and photographs provided by the Wetherill family remain the best evidence of discovery.

Even though I believe some of the reports of earlier sightings or examinations of Cliff Palace, there is no physical evidence – either inscriptions or documentation – to thoroughly support those claims. Ultimately, being the first to *see* Cliff Palace really isn't the issue. It was what the Wetherills *did* to document what they examined at – and removed from – the cliff dwellings that mattered, and may be the best reason to continue giving them credit for the discovery.

Many adventurers saw, explored, and excavated the cliff dwellings of the Mancos Canyon before them, but the Wetherills were the first to focus on preservation and use a scientific approach for excavation. They resepcted and wanted to learn from what they found, not merely profit from it. Guided by the Inward Light of their being, they knew the difference.

EPILOGUE

J esse Nusbaum, Mesa Verde park superintendent, in 1930 attempt- ed to sort out individual archaeological collections assembled by the Wetherill brothers. He struggled to link collections with each Wetherill storie into the canyon of the Mancos. I also will attempt to describe collections gathered by the Wetherills, using the work of Nusbaum and present-day researcher Ann Phillips, of Boulder, Colorado, who spent much of her team effort on the Wetherill/Grand Gulch Project identifying collections and their current locations. Undoubtedly, in the early years from 1885 to 1888 before the sponsorship of major museums, collections were sold to individuals, a common practice throughout the Four Corners.

1. July of 1885-1888: Excavations at the Brownstone Front (Hemenway House 2, close to Balcony House) initiated Wetherill family collecting within the cliff dwellings. They are followed by a collection sold to Helen and James Chain in 1887.

2. December 18, 1888: A small collection of artifacts, including a stone ax with handle described by Charlie Mason in 1917, collect- ed in Cliff Palace following Richard and Charlie's sighting of the dwelling.

3. December 1888 through March 1889: Excavation led by Charles McLoyd in Cliff Palace, Spruce Tree House, and Square Tower House. Collection taken to Denver and sold by McLoyd for $3,000 to the Colorado State Historical Society with the help of Mrs. Helen Henderson Chain, friend of William Henry Jackson.

4. Spring of 1889 up to Nordenskiöld visit in 1891: Wetherill brothers begin independent work gathering collections. Excav- ations likely start at Sandal House. Frederick Chapin photographs this site in detail on his first trip to the cliff dwellings. This is the most thorough search and collection conducted exclusively by all the Wetherill brothers and Charlie Mason. This collection is the core – with some additional items collected in 1891 and 1892 – of what is sent to the Minneapolis Exposition and later to the World's Columbian Exposition in Chicago in 1893. Sponsorship of the exhibits was provided by C.D. Hazzard under the guidance of H.J. Smith.

5. Summer of 1891: Collection completed by Gustaf Nordenskiöld and John Wetherill for shipment to Sweden. Much of the excavation completed in canyons draining off of the Wetherill Mesa in Mesa Verde National Park. Results in the arrest of Gustaf Nordenskiöld in Durango at the request of Indian Agent

Charles Bartholomew. Charges subsequently dismissed and collections shipped to Sweden, catalogued, published, and currently at the Finland National Museum.

6. Summer of 1892: Last collection made by the Wetherill brothers. Results in their arrest by Sheriff Adam Lewey under complaint by Charles Bartholomew. Charges subsequently dismissed. In addition to adding to the collection Richard and his family wished to send to the World's Columbian Exposition, they assist A.F. Willmarth in the excavation of artifacts for the Colorado Exhibit at the same exposition in Chicago.

7. The 1904 collections sold at the St. Louis World's Fair now reside in Berlin, Germany, and the Chicago Field Museum. Neither collection is yet identified as to origin.

Three of the six Mesa Verde collections above are usually attributed to the Wetherill brothers when in fact they were assembled at the direction of other individuals. They are the McLoyd, Nordenskiöld, and Willmarth collections. It is difficult to determine where the contents of three of the remaining four collections ended up, but the Wetherills clearly were selling artifact collections and individual pieces, to representatives or expedition sponsors representing reputable museums.

* * *

The Wetherill family did much more than archaeological pioneering. Richard, according to local newspaper articles, accompanied a group to excavate a Stegosaur fossil along the Colorado-Utah border. Al helped Alice Eastwood discover rare plants. John pioneered trail routes and a Western movie industry with his wife Louisa. John worked hard for the National Park Service in northeastern Arizona, while Louisa established personal relationships with Navajo and Ute people, aiding cultural progress while documenting ethnobotanical and cultural beliefs. This is what made the family such a valuable resource to scientists and a sought-after source for visitors long after their departure from the Alamo Ranch.

Wetherill family expeditions into the Four Corners exemplify horse riding and packing skills. Minor accidents to clients and themselves with no fatalities or debilitating injury is remarkable. Serious conflicts with Native Americans were never recorded. Many photographs show sidearms being worn by the brothers. John and Clayton's photograph is for show and advertising purposes. Wearing sidearms on the trail was then and is now essential for dispatching fatally injured or ill horses, defending against wild animals, or obtaining food. Win and Richard were known as skilled marksmen, yet no mention in the historical record has them using sidearms in

Richard Wetherill's Trading Post in Chaco.

conflict with their fellow man.

John and Louisa Wetherill had two natural children and three adopted children. Their daughter Georgia Ida was killed in a tragic traffic accident in the mid-1930s leaving her two daughters Johni Lou and Dorothy. John and Louisa also adopted three Navajo girls. Betty Zane, named after author Zane Grey, Fannie and Esther who died of tuberculosis. Fannie and Esther were children of Navajo leader Hoskinini. John's son Ben Wetherill helped John on many of his archaeological expeditions while leading few of his own. Ben took a crew of Navajos to the Aleutians during World War II even though he had lost an eye in a horse accident, and destroyed a leg in a gun accident. His skills in their language, as well as his ability to supervise Navajos, were in demand by the military.

Harvey Leake, great-grandson of John Wetherill, is currently compiling a detailed biography of the lives of John and Louisa Wetherill.

Richard Wetherill died in Chaco Canyon on June 22, 1910. The official version named Chis Chilling Begay, a Navajo who spent five years in prison for the murder, as the assassin. While in prison he contracted tuberculosis and was released for medical reasons.

However, more was at work than the bullet fired by Begay. A combination of events converged into a single flash point that ended the life of Richard Wetherill. Three shots were reportedly fired at Richard or Bill Finn, his suspect ranch hand. Finn provoked the incident by pistol-whipping Begay for stealing a colt belonging to Richard's daughter Elizabeth.

Richard, as always, was traveling unarmed when the shooting occurred.

The first shot, according to Finn, the only eyewitness to the murder, missed its mark; the second went through Richard's hand and into his chest. The third was fired at close range, hitting Richard in the head. Who fired that third shot is a mystery, but the hired hand remains suspect. Marietta Wetherill later married Bill Finn in Bernalillo, New Mexico. He reportedly died of pneumonia on a rail trip east, leaving Marietta once again a widow.

Marietta later told historian McNitt that the day Richard was shot, Finn rode into the trading post at a gallop, pursued by a Navajo, Joe Yazzie. Eleanor Quick, tutor for the Wetherill children, stated that Finn rode in *with* the Navajos.

Unsure of possible reprisal, Navajo warriors quickly prepared for retaliation from the trading post. They painted their faces for war, then posted themselves on the cliffs above the Wetherill Trading Post. When retaliation failed to materialize they disbanded.

Richard's eldest son, Richard II, recalled the painted Navajo warriors on the cliff surrounding the trading post. He posted himself at a window, cradling a rifle, his arm resting on a Navajo rug he had hacked to pieces with a hatchet as a child of six when his parents left without him on a short trip. Upset at being left behind, he had mutilated the rug. Marietta, upon her return, mended the weaving on her Singer sewing machine, then attempted to dye the patches to match the original rug. He kept the mended rug and it still resides in family archives today.

Marietta was forced to leave the trading post after Richard's death, sending a load of horses east to raise cash to move to a homestead in the mountains near Cuba, New Mexico. Communication with the rest of the Wetherill family diminished to a rare Christmas card or quick note. Al and John would track the children, but close contact with Marietta ended.

Whatever the circumstances, Richard's death left a lasting multigenerational mark upon his family. Elizabeth blamed herself for her father's death, while her brother Richard II assumed leadership as the eldest son. He felt driven throughout his life to care for his siblings and would, in 1965, organize the first Wetherill family reunion. Aided by Jack Wade, who was Louisa Wetherill's nephew and by then chief ranger at Mesa Verde National Park, Richard II accomplished the first gathering of the Wetherill family since their final departure from the Alamo Ranch in 1902.

* * *

John, Al, Richard, Clayton, Anna, and Charlie Mason's stories told herein describe early archaeology in the Southwest. Their pioneer efforts after leaving the Alamo Ranch are only touched on here, but will be continued in a subsequent publication. Contributions by their family to archaeology, anthropology, ethnobotany, ethnography and the communities in which they chose to live go well beyond their years exploring the Mesa Verde. The

Wren Wetherill Scarberry with quiver reportedly found in Cliff Palace and Al's glass plate camera used in Mesa Verde.

Wetherill brothers chose to quietly, unpretentiously explore the remnants of Ancestral Puebloans. Scholarly study of that exploration is long overdue.

Mysteries and connection to artifacts believed once to have been in the possession of the Wetherill family remain in folklore similar to stories of lost or hidden gold. Within the Wetherill Family Archives is a prehistoric quiver, approximately 53 cm long and 11 cm wide. Fourteen projectile points of the Pueblo III era tied by yucca twine in a special knotting are highly visible on the leather pouch.

Patched with several pieces of leather of unknown origin, the quiver is an enigma. Wetherill family oral history suggests it came from cliff dwellings in the Mesa Verde and very likely Cliff Palace, yet the written record of such a discovery is, so far, absent. Perhaps a thorough search of written material in the Wetherill Family Archives will solve the riddle.

A large collection of artifacts removed by Richard Wetherill, Charlie Mason, Wirt Jenks Billings, and Roe Ethridge from the canyons and cliff dwelling of Navajo National Monument and Marsh Pass in 1895 remains missing. Clues exist to both what this supposed wagonload of 400 pieces of pottery included – reportedly southwestern polychrome and white-on-black wares – and where it ended up.

Intrinisic and economic values are placed upon artifacts believed to have originated from the Wetherill family. One example is a well-made Mesa Verdean mug, believed to have been discovered by John Wetherill while excavating at Mug House on Wetherill Mesa during the 1890s. At one point the mug was presented to a major collector of artifacts from Oklahoma. His daughter inherited it, later moving to Twentynine Palms in California, where she gave it to an artist. The "Wetherill" mug was eventually bought by a man who now wishes to understand provenience and perhaps donate the artifact back to a curatorial facility near where it was discovered.

A large Wetherill collection, primarily of Navajo rugs, jewelry, and documents of the historic period was donated by the Wetherill family to a major New Mexico museum in trust for the family, only to disappear. Yet, rugs from the collection are reappearing in private collections with the Wetherill name attached.

* * *

The scientific community must not ignore the power of avocational involvement in understanding all aspects of science. Scientific interest is not exclusive to higher degrees of education. We, as professionals in our fields, need to listen to those voices.

— **Fred M. Blackburn**

A Note on Sources

References for this publication are derived from three primary sources: the Anasazi Heritage Center Wetherill Family Archives, and personal archives in possession of Harvey Leake and Fred Blackburn.

Of the three sources the Wetherill Family Archives curated at the Bureau of Land Management Anasazi Heritage Center, Dolores, Colorado, has provided the bulk of the detail and the humanity to this publication. Approximately 11,000 items exist in 12 different accessions as the backbone of the Wetherill Family Archives. Of those 11,000 items, approximately 1,500 have a final accession number and permanent archive location at this time. For that reason, an exact citation by archive catalog number is impossible at this time for most of the references in this text.

Harvey Leake and Fred Blackburn have extensive libraries and files of material accumulated over the past 30 years. Newspaper information is from Blackburn's data base of nearly 2,300 newspaper and magazine sources. Many of those are primary sources or copies of primary sources presented as resource gifts to the author without detailed citation. Personal communication from Wetherill family members and others is used infrequently but presents itself within this text. Both collections are hoped to reside eventually the Bureau of Land Management Anasazi Heritage Center Wetherill Archives.

Many of Blackburn's files have accumulated from other institutions such as the Mesa Verde National Park Research Lab, Smithsonian Institution, National Archives, Museum of Northern Arizona, Arizona State University, Animas Museum, Center of Southwest Studies at Fort Lewis College, Denver Public Library, and Colorado State Historical Society, to mention but a few. They are cited as the origination point for primary research when appropriate.

John Richardson, retired professor from Southern Illinois University, made innumerable contributions through his unpublished anthology of archaeological exploration of the Four Corners and primary photographs.

SUGGESTIONS FOR
FURTHER READING

Reference material described in this publication is found scattered in other publications as well. Several of the credible publications are listed as suggested reading within this text. Most notable is Frank McNitt's *Richard Wetherill: Anasazi*. In 1957 McNitt worked from oral histories of the surviving people who had been directly involved in archaeological discovery.

I worked from the primary documents of the Wetherill family, many of them sources which were also available to McNitt in 1957. I also worked from research compiled from inscription documentation and newspaper research as well as other available sources. My hope is that this work agrees, compliments, and adds to the telling of the Wetherill story.

The following reading list is provided for readers interested in other information written about the Wetherill family and "the Boys."

Anasazi Basketmaker: Papers from the 1990 Wetherill/Grand Gulch Symposium. Published in 1993 by the Utah Bureau of Land Management; *Anasazi Basketmaker* explores the work of the Wetherill Grand Gulch Project and scholars with an interest in Ancestral Puebloan Basketmaker. Editor Victoria Atkins; authors include Fred Blackburn, Winston Hurst, and Christy Turner.

Around Hogan Fires. scheduled for publication by Gibbs Smith Publishers in 2006; completed as a manuscript by Louisa Wetherill in the early 1930s, with a recent forward by Harvey Leake, her great-grandson. An oral history translated by Louisa from Navajo mentor Wolf Killer explores the wisdom of the Navajo.

Butch Cassidy Was Here. Written by James Knipmeyer and published by the University of Utah Press in 2002. The book is an excellent example of the use of inscription "graffiti" as a primary research document.

Cliff Dwellers of the Mesa Verde. Published by Gustaf Nordenskiöld in 1893. A most thorough study for its time, published in Swedish and English. Original versions of this text are rare, but it has been re-released twice, by Rio Grande Press and Mesa Verde Museum Association. John Wetherill made the notes for Nordenskiöld's work.

Cowboys and Cave Dwellers. Published in 1997 by the School of American Research; explores the role of the Wetherill brothers in the early exploration for the Basketmaker. Authors are Fred Blackburn and Ray Williamson.

Desert Wife. Hilda Faunce, second wife of Winslow Wetherill, wrote *Desert Wife*, published in 1928, as an examination of her and Winslow's life while traders at Black Mountain in northeastern Arizona. Names are left anonymous or changed in the text.

Land of the Cliff Dwellers. Published in 1892; author Frederick Chapin was the first to explore the findings of Richard Wetherill in Mesa Verde. Photographs reveal what many of the dwellings visited by the Wetherills looked like when they first visited them. Richard Wetherill provided much of the information to Chapin.

Rainbow To Yesterday. Published in 1980; Mary Comfort provides another view of the life of John and Louisa Wetherill while living in Kayenta, Arizona. Many investigative errors found in this text, but it nonetheless provides an insight into their time in Kayenta.

Richard Wetherill, Anasazi. First published by the University of New Mexico Press in 1957, this publication has remained in print. A classic for those interested in the Wetherills, it focuses primarily on Richard and Marietta Wetherill. Author Frank McNitt made few errors in his detailed research of their lives in Southwest archaeology.

Ruins and Rivals, The Making of Southwest Archaeology. Published by the University of Arizona Press in 2001. Author James Snead provides a glimpse into the hidden world of archaeological rivalries in the Southwest during the era of the Wetherill brothers. An excellent backroom view of the formulation of Southwestern archaeology.

Stones Speak and Waters Sing: The Life and Works of Gustaf Nordenskiöld. Published in 1984; written by Olaf W. Arrhenius (grandson of Gustaf Nordenskiöld) and edited by Robert H. and Florence Lister; this publication reviews exploration of the Mesa Verde and the Grand Canyon by Gustaf Nordenskiöld and the Wetherill brothers in 1891. Well-written and well-illustrated with photographs.

Traders to the Navajos. Published in 1952; co-authored by Frances Gillmor and Louisa Wade Wetherill, *Traders* explores the history of John and Louisa Wetherill. Emphasis is placed on their life together in Kayenta, Arizona.

The Wetherills of the Mesa Verde: Autobiography of Benjamin Alfred Wetherill. Edited by Maureen Fletcher and published in 1973; this text provides a revealing history, based on Al's writings. Out of print and may be difficult to find.

The Wetherill family web page is hosted by Jimmy Shaffner, the grandson of Richard Wetherill, at http://wetherillfamily.com.

INDEX

I-K

L

M

We appreciate your business!